BETTING ON
RED

Winning True Peace, Hope, and
Happiness with One Simple Bet on Red

SHAWN WARD

ISBN 978-1-0980-3104-6 (paperback)
ISBN 978-1-0980-3105-3 (digital)

Christian Faith Publishing, Inc.
832 Park Avenue
Meadville, PA 16335
www.christianfaithpublishing.com

Printed in the United States of America

Robynn—My beautiful bride, best friend, and an amazing mother. I love you!

Emma and Nate—The best children a mom and dad could ever have. You bring so much joy to everyone around you. We love you and are so proud of you!

Ariana—I can't thank you enough for all your encouragement. You and Bella are so talented. Don't stop creating!

CONTENTS

FOREWORD

My wife Autumn and I have had the privilege of serving our community and pastoring Anthem Church in Long Beach, California. This is where we met Shawn. After getting to know him, it's unbelievable that this joy-filled man almost committed suicide over 20 years ago. His story and journey have been an inspiration to many and I believe God has placed this special message on his heart to help people who are searching for more in life just like he was.

There are a lot of self-development books out there that promote peace, joy, and fulfillment in life. However, none are like Betting On Red. I've served in full-time ministry all over the country and met so many people in search of peace in their lives. I wish that I would have found this book sooner as an additional resource to recommend to everyone I talked to in search of true peace. In Betting On Red, Shawn offers such practical and encouraging news for hearts that are lost, troubled and searching for real peace, hope, and happiness in their lives. This book presents the Good News of Jesus in a fresh way that will breathe new life to anyone out there in search of something more. I truly hope that all who read this book will end up betting on red; for they will never lose.

Pastor Daniel Katz
Lead Pastor, Anthem Church
Long Beach, California
www.theanthemchurch.com
Daniel@theanthemchurch.com
Autumn@theanthemchurch.com
@anthemchurchlb

PREFACE

You're twenty-one years old, and you've been waiting for this moment your entire life.

You've been driving down this dark desert highway for about three hours now, and you're almost there. The pent-up excitement for this very moment has caused many sleepless nights. Your heart begins to thump out of your chest as you creep around the final turn in the desert road. The weariness from the long drive quickly becomes a distant memory as you catch your first glimpse of the city.

You exchange the dark, dreary desert road for a cascade of brilliant light that flooded the midnight sky. You're in complete awe as you pull into town and begin to see things you had seen only in the movies before now. The streets are jam-packed with entertainers, taxis, limousines, low-riders, and party buses. There's an electrifying buzz in the air like nothing you've ever felt before. It's a summer Saturday night, and you're on the Las Vegas strip for the first time.

You turn into the hottest hotel-casino on the boulevard and check-in at the desk. Glancing up, you can't help but notice the thirty-foot gold-leaf painted ceilings, elegant chandeliers, and draperies that appear to be imported from a distant land. Looking around, you can't help but see people from all over the globe swarm around the hall, looking hot and dressed to impress. Your senses are on overload as you see the flashing lights and crowds pressing around the slot machines and card tables while the servers keep the drinks flowing. You smell the aroma of cigars, men's cologne, and women's perfume saturating every inch of airspace as you keep wandering through.

Walking toward the elevator to your room, you notice a large crowd around one particular roulette table and abruptly change course. As you walk closer to the table, you stand up on your toes to see over the crowd and catch a glimpse of the action. "What's going on here?" you ask the lady standing by your side.

"This nut job just bet $77 million on the color red. If it lands on red, he wins an extra $77 million, but if it lands on black, he loses it all. This guy has lost his mind!" The silence around the table is astonishing. They all hold their breaths, watching the little ball bounce around as the wheel spins in anticipation to find out what color the ball lands on.

The high roller betting the wager isn't worried at all. This man happens to know without a doubt that the ball will land on red. Why? Well, minutes before the gambler left his hotel room, he was looking for his room key and opened the nightstand drawer. Much to his surprise, he found two gifts left by the maker of the roulette wheel.

One gift was a small booklet. He opened it, and what he saw made him almost pass out. This little book gave the reader step-by-step instructions to make any roulette wheel land on red with pin-point accuracy, resulting in doubling his money from a single spin. This booklet not only gave him directions, but also a second gift—a deposit check with a portion of the winnings proving there was substantially more to come.

To the crowds watching this guy at the roulette table, it appears he has completely lost his mind to bet that much money. However, what appears to be a gamble is no gamble at all. Winning is guaranteed. His bet will assure his initial investment back—with an extra $77 million in return. All he has to do is trust the maker of the roulette wheel, lay down his chips, and receive the prize. One small element of trust, combined with a ton of evidence that is backed up with a deposit guarantee.

At the same table, six spots to the left of this man is a world-renowned psychic with phenomenal luck at a roulette table. Being a psychic, she usually has a following of other players copying her bets. The crowd is excited to see the psychic in on this round of insane betting. She throws all her chips in on black. The other players have never witnessed her betting like that before. Thinking she has a serious premonition, they also throw in all their chips on black in hopes of doubling their money.

In the scene before us, every person at the table bets everything they have because the thought of missing out is too much to bear. The player betting on red is equipped with a step-by-step guide and a guarantee, while the other players bet on black because of the psychic's intrigue and confidence. With the room in suspense, the wheel slows down, and the ball comes to a stop. It lands on red. Emotional devastation rips through the crowd as they stare in disbelief. Red is victorious—as promised.

Rewinding time a bit will reveal something else important to know. The other players at the table were not aware they had the same opportunity to win as this guy did. The maker of the roulette game had put a little booklet in everyone's hotel room. If they had looked in their nightstands, they would have found the same instructions. Unfortunately for them, they rushed away from their rooms and ignored the amazing gift left for them.

If you and I had been sitting at that roulette table betting that round, how would we have bet? Would we have followed the other players, driven by the false confidence and intrigue of someone who thought they knew the future—or would we have followed the man who bet on red who got his instructions from the maker? Had we taken the time to look in the nightstand as the man had, we would be betting with him.

This analogy is highly symbolic but based on truth. We all sit at a table surrounded by lots of noise and flashing lights. It's not a roulette table, but very similar—it's the table of life. We sit back at the table and watch the wheel spin around and around, watching our lives go by day after day, just waiting to lay our chips down and make a bet. The chips we lay down represent what we trust in and give our lives to in hopes of winning the jackpot we all want—lasting peace, hope, and happiness from deep within.

As we journey through life, we are either actively or passively searching for what will satisfy the natural spiritual hunger in our lives. Like hunting for that missing puzzle piece, we seem to be on a secret mission to find fulfilling happiness, security, contentment, and rest. As the wheel of life spins around in circles and days go by, we look at a variety of things to place our bets on to fulfill our search. We look around thinking the missing piece will be found in relationships, philosophies, material things, ideas, spirituality, and even religiosity. Unfortunately, these bets on black leave us feeling unfulfilled time and time again.

Unaware that the answer is right there in our nightstand, we glance around the table of life and listen to what everybody has to say before we make our next bet. Society has a point of view and our friends and family have their own. Neighbors, news media, the intellectual, and the successful all have their own ideas on how to fill the natural void in our hearts. We find something that initially sounds good, so we lay our chips down and bet on it, hoping for the best. When it doesn't fulfill as we had hoped, we move on and look for the next…and that cycle repeats itself. I know this all too well to be true because this is how it happened for me.

I tried to put a smile on for the world, but truthfully, I felt incomplete on the inside. Something huge was missing in my life. I couldn't quite put my finger on what it was, but the void annoyed me to the core. The time finally came when enough was enough. I had to choose one of two options immediately: find the reason for the emptiness…or simply decide to end it all.

I began searching and seeking like never before. Suddenly, almost like stumbling on a winning lottery ticket, I found the jackpot lying right in front of my face. It had been hiding in plain sight, but I just didn't have the eyes to see it. It was step-by-step instructions on how to make a winning bet, resulting in an overflowing amount of exactly what I had been looking for. It was a treasure map that led to a lasting peace so liberating, that I couldn't help but write the secrets down in this book to help others find the same radical hope that millions of us who have bet on red experience year after year.

How do you place your bets on red and discover the priceless treasure of true peace, joy, hope, and happiness for the rest of your life? It's all in the instruction manual. There is a step-by-step guide that is guaranteed to give you victory. It's guaranteed because it is written by the Maker—the Maker of life itself. This bet will take one small element of belief, combined with a whole lot of evidence, backed up with a gift as a deposit guaranteeing the bet will win as promised.

I will begin to break down what red means and how to make a winning bet as we move through the chapters of this book. The exciting thing is that our Maker gave us amazing insight and told us how to pick the winner with one hundred percent certainty. It's all written in his little book in the hotel nightstand that we rarely read. Not only does he tell us to bet on red, but when we do, the bet will pay *enormous* dividends. The payoff will be so huge that we're promised our minds cannot fully comprehend how amazing it will be.

There is great news for players sitting at the table of life. If you are reading this, you still have time to win a monumental victory that leaves hopelessness in your dust as you enter a life of hope, joy, and purpose forevermore.

I'd like to show you a small glimpse of the darkness that ruled my world over twenty years ago so you can know where I'm coming from. I went "all in" with the bet on black, but my attempts to find peace were all futile. As you will see shortly, my life-altering discovery is unbelievably simple to replicate. My hope and prayer for everyone reading this is that you too will bet on red and become rich beyond your wildest dreams!

INTRODUCTION

It was a cool Friday night at "the house." The sounds of Sublime, Beastie Boys and Rage Against the Machine blasted against every wall. The house was the ultimate party pad. Alcohol flowed like a river and there was no shortage of my drug of choice. I remember hanging out on the back patio feeling pretty numb. I had taken down about seven beers by that time and was flying high. The blaring music was just one more layer of distraction to help me forget the world around me just one more time…and it was always that, *just one more time.*

I really needed nights like this, nights to get plastered enough to forget about the negativity, emptiness, and despair that walked with me like a close friend. Nobody suspected a thing, and I wanted to keep it that way. It seemed to me that everyone was in the same boat that I was, washing away the pain with any thrill or substance that would do the job.

My high started to wear off a little, so it was time to go home. I hopped into my tattered 1967 VW bug and blasted my music for all the neighbors to hear. As I was driving off, panic and fear struck me as never before. Funny, because just two hours earlier, I had been free as a bird with no problem in the world. My eyes locked into my rearview mirror. Completely petrified, I kept murmuring to myself, "Oh God, I'm beyond drunk and high. If I get pulled over, it's jail time for sure…good job Shawn."

Paranoid, I pulled over to the side of the road to make sure no cops were tailing me. The coast seemed clear, so I pulled out and headed down Bellflower Boulevard to my home in Lakewood, California. I remember saying to myself, "What the heck am I doing? I will never drive drunk or high ever again."

Well, thankfully I made it home that night, but I never kept that promise I had made to myself. I drove drunk and high plenty of times after that. I knew I had to start facing my demons, but they seemed to be growing beyond my ability to contain. What had started as a baby depression growing within me had evolved into a full-size adult by the end of my senior year of high school.

I grew increasingly empty and more and more depressed as each day passed. I couldn't quite pinpoint why I felt so incomplete. Was it the rough early childhood, the drug abuse I had been exposed to as a kid, the poor personal choices I had made? Or was this just the way the world was? Whatever it was, I couldn't help but wonder why I was living in this cruel world and if my life had any purpose.

Uninvited thoughts of negativity, doubt, confusion, and fear poured through my mind for no reason at all. Life sucked. I concluded that the only way to relieve the sadness was to take my own life—and do it quickly. Day after day I thought of different ways I could kill myself that wouldn't be too gruesome to whoever found me.

One night I had a vivid dream I still remember today. I had put a red bandana on my head to hide the blood when I pulled the trigger of a gun I was about to buy. The next night, I bought a red bandana like the one I had seen in my dream and went home. It was late at night, and I didn't know where to buy a gun, so I hunted through my roommate's room for one. I looked everywhere but came up empty. I was so tired and drained from all this internal drama, I just hit the bed and crashed.

That night I had another vivid dream that was the beginning of my turning point. I was running through a dark alley being chased by guys who weren't any good. I don't remember why they were chasing me, but I was running as fast as I could. As I was running, I looked ahead and saw a light piercing through the pitch-black alley. It seemed to be a store of some sort. I remember running and diving for the light. I woke up drenched in sweat from head to toe.

The next morning, I forced myself to go to class. I was halfway through a class at a local community college that taught principles of success in life. Showing up every day was my only hope for finding the answers I needed for some sort of direction in my life; desperately hoping it would lead to some form of happiness.

I will remember a certain day in class for the rest of my life. The instructor was teaching on our mental willpower, our psyche, and what motivates us to make good decisions in life. I'm not sure how it happened, but she got on a tangent about dreams, their meaning, and interpretation. She said she had interpreted several dreams in the past and asked the class if anyone wanted to share a dream and have it interpreted. I reluctantly raised my hand and told her the dream.

After I had shared, she looked at me and said, "It seems that you may be running from something very dark, and you are trying to find peace. That store's light may have represented the peace and happiness you are searching for." She exposed everything going on inside me. I was embarrassed. Now the entire class knew the battle that raged within my weary soul.

The feeling of hopelessness seemed to find its way through the chambers of my heart at the most inopportune times. As I sat there embarrassed, I couldn't help but notice my classmates giggling at me because of my dream, and I decided that enough was enough. I used my last ounce of energy to storm out of the classroom and find a quiet place to lie down and consider my next move.

I found a huge grassy field, flung my backpack to the ground and laid flat on my back, staring at the sky. Feeling a sudden urge to pray, I looked up and tried talking to God for the first time in a long time. I didn't know much about God or what he wanted from me, but I knew deep down inside that he existed. At that moment, somehow I knew he was the only one who had the power to take away my pain. I prayed, "If you're up there God, I need your help. I can't go on anymore." As the words of that prayer left my mouth, I felt a strange temporary peace I'd never felt before. It was like a stay of execution. I drove home in awe of what had just happened.

A few days passed, and I had an urge to go and see my mom, whom I didn't see very often. Visits to my mom's side of the family were pretty infrequent, probably because of the rough memories I had as a kid. As we talked, she mentioned that my aunt Patty also wanted me to visit, after what seemed to be years of not seeing my mom's side of the family. For some reason, I felt safe with her and wanted to see her as soon as possible. I hopped in the car and drove straight over there, not realizing that I was soon to find the answer to all my misery.

I got to my aunt's single-wide trailer in Downey, California, about three o'clock that afternoon in July of 1997. I walked up to her doorstep and saw an overjoyed woman waiting for me with the biggest bear hug I've had in years. We walked inside, and she said, "Let me look at you. I have missed you so much." She put her warm hands on my tense shoulders. "Come and sit down. I have to talk to you."

As we sat there in her trailer, I couldn't shake the amazing comforting feeling of joy that radiated from her like electricity. She began to utter words that changed the rest of my life. "Shawn," she said, "God loves you very much. He sent you here so I can tell you that." I began to bawl like a baby. She had no idea what I had been through and how close I was to suicide.

As she talked to me about how much God loves me, I felt overwhelming waves of love, peace, and joy flood over me, nearly bringing me to my knees. I stopped her in her tracks and told her what I was feeling and asked her what was going on. She answered, "God is showing you that he loves you and that he is very real."

We sat for hours talking about what God had done for her and what she had been through. She told me a story of a car wreck she had been in. Paraphrasing her story, she was crossing an intersection and got hit in the side by a speeding car, throwing her car into a telephone pole. When the paramedics arrived, they found her dead in the driver's seat. After quickly assessing her, they put a sheet over her mangled body as they waited for the coroner.

She remembers waking up and walking through a tunnel-like structure with a brilliant light at the end. She saw my grandmother and her brother Ricky, who had died at the age of five, waving at her. As she walked closer, she realized they were waving at her to go back. She wanted to keep going into the light but realized that wasn't going to happen. They waved her back the other way because God had other plans for her.

She awoke from her few moments at the gate of heaven and found a sheet over her face. She pulled it down with what strength she could muster and tried to cry for help. The paramedics, shocked and amazed, rushed to her aid. That day, everyone saw a true modern-day miracle.

My aunt told me many more stories after that of how God had radically helped her. My initial thought was this was simply not possible. But the tangible presence of something supernatural happening within me in conjunction with the physical waves of joy and peace that invaded my soul made it really hard to refute what she was telling me. You could say I became an instant believer in the spiritual realm even though I couldn't see it with my own eyes.

For three solid weeks, I frequently visited my aunt to hear about this God she loved so much. I knew I needed what she had, and I was determined to find out how to get a dose of this heavenly high she was on. One particular day, I drove to get her some cough medicine from the store because she was fighting a cold. I spotted a liquor store and tried to turn left into the parking lot. Heavy traffic wouldn't allow me to make the turn, so I went to the end of the block to turn around.

As I approached the next street I could turn on, I felt a gentle, but strong whisper say to me, "Stay here." I didn't know what to think of this comforting, but powerful command. Accompanying this calming voice, I felt a physical presence of something peaceful and beautiful all around me. It was very bizarre in an amazing way. I couldn't see anyone there, and frankly, I was afraid to see anyone if they were there. I pulled over and just waited, not knowing what I was waiting for.

I began to think I was crazy for sitting on this side street and convinced myself I hadn't heard anything. I pulled out to drive away and get back to my mission to find some cough syrup. As I began to turn and leave the street, an exterior garage light at the corner house rapidly flickered on and off as if it were trying to get my attention. I knew this was a sign of some sort that I needed to stay there. I turned back around and just waited in bewilderment.

Several moments passed, and I began to sense the same powerful feeling of God's Spirit all around me. Physical waves of love, joy, and peace grew stronger and stronger every second that went by. Overwhelmed with tears of joy, I just closed my eyes and began thanking God for these refreshing emotions that paralyzed me for a brief moment in time. I opened my eyes to discover a little orange and white cat, slowly approaching the brightness of my headlights that pierced through that darkness of that summer night. I couldn't take my eyes off of it.

As the cat came closer, the feeling of God's Spirit got stronger and stronger. It stopped in front of the hood of my car and stared me down for at least twenty seconds. The longer the cat looked at me, the presence of God's Spirit flooded over me, filling me with more and more physical waves of love and joy. I closed my eyes and began whispering in amazement, "Thank you, God." I opened my eyes once more. The cat walked away, and the comforting presence slowly faded. I sat there speechless, wondering what had just happened.

I pulled away from that street, bought my aunt's medicine, returned to her place, and told her about what had just happened to me. She reiterated that God was trying to reveal himself to me and show me that he truly loved me; after all, that's what I had asked for in the big field just days before.

The next morning on the drive home, I went by that little street near Downey, California. To my absolute amazement, it was called Angell Street, with two L's for some reason. It all hit me at that point that God was sending an angel in the form of a little kitty cat to show me that he was there, that he truly existed and was trying to help me. It was surreal.

Many more supernatural things happened to me over the course of the next few weeks. It became obvious to me that there is a supernatural world out there available for anyone to tap into if they just seek and ask for help. I had asked God for help in the past, but it was only to get me out of some sort of trouble. Once I was out of trouble, I paid no attention to him. He was my convenience-store God.

After all these amazing events, I started going to church, paying money to the church, and doing all things religious, not knowing what to do next. Little did I know—I was still missing the most important part of this journey that would soon cause my whole life to turn upside down in the best way possible.

A few days later, I realized I was going to be out of town on a certain Sunday and wouldn't be able to go to church. I took a midweek drive to the church to give an offering in place of my absence. A block shy of the church building, I blew right past a stop sign and turned left onto Ardmore Ave. A low-rider came barreling toward me at a high rate of speed and almost side-swiped me. I turned my wheel sharply and barely missed him.

I quickly glanced over and looked the driver in the eye to see the most-wicked look I've ever seen on a human being's face. I had always known this was gangbanger territory but never had any issues before. I sped away in fear for my life and parked at the church. I was so shaken up when I got there, I had forgotten why I was there in the first place.

I knocked on the door and asked, "Is Pastor Van Schepen here?" Mrs. Van Schepen directed me to the chapel next door. My heart racing, I walked across the driveway, and the low-rider stopped right out front, just staring me down. I yelled out that I was sorry; thankfully, he drove away.

All shaken up, I approached a small office off the chapel and looked inside. Pastor John Van Schepen was sitting at his desk. He said, "How can I help you?" I was so shaken up, I couldn't say a word. The pastor stared at me for about three seconds and promptly walked over to his wall and pulled out a small booklet from a brochure holder. He handed it to me. "Take this home and read it, son."

The title of the booklet was, *The Road to Peace*. The second this little book hit my shaking hands, I knew I was holding the missing piece to the incomplete puzzle of events that was happening in my life. For some reason, I knew this was the end of all the depression, doubt, confusion, and fear. All that was left to do was get to a quiet place and start reading. I left Pastor Van Schepen's office and drove home as fast as I could. I ran inside the house, hopped into my recliner, and began to read.

The opening of the booklet was a picture of two cities separated from each other by a seemingly endless black hole. The city on the left looked like a dark and dreary metropolitan city, while the one on the right was an amazing city of gold and light—symbolizing the separation between heaven and earth.

There were several incomplete bridges that were obviously failed attempts at connecting the two cities. Each bridge had a name. One was "good deeds." Another was "I was a good person." Yet another "religion," and the final one "I'm not that bad of a person." None of the bridges even came close to connecting earth to heaven.

By the end of this little booklet, I saw another bridge. This one was different. It was strong, stable, and complete—all the way to the other side. It wasn't built by human hands but by the hand of Jesus himself. This little booklet showed me step by step how to find this bridge, cross it, and receive the treasure waiting for me. I was amazed by how simple it was.

That summer afternoon in 1997, I got down on my knees and accepted God's invitation for peace in my life and bet everything I had on red. The incredible heavy burden of life, depression, and confusion left my body in an instant and an overwhelming comfort, joy, and peace flowed through my veins like electricity. However, this time it was permanent.

Now, over twenty years later, life has only gotten better and the peace has only intensified. It was mind-blowing to me that it happened so quickly and naturally—more importantly, that it was so easily duplicated for anyone out there in search of this kind of hope and happiness in their life.

Ten years ago, I felt a strong urge to pick up my laptop and started writing this book in hopes to convey this simple message so that everyone out there can experience this kind of liberation that millions of us who bet on red have experienced. If you're anything like me, you'll be so excited to finally see, feel, and live this new and improved version of life.

My attempt at conveying the betting on red message had to start with some self-analyzation of how I first received the information. I asked myself, *Shawn, what were the first steps that you took to find this amount of hope and freedom and how would you convey it to others in order for them to experience the same?* The answer was threefold. First, one would have to be prepared to receive the information. I'm talking about being completely open to ideas that may seem unfamiliar. Second, would be a tremendous hunger and thirst for the truth—so much so, that you would read this book all the way through.

If you're open and on a serious hunt for an everlasting peace that never fails, you are right on track and about to hit the jackpot. If you are not serious about it—I wouldn't read any further until you've reached that point.

Once someone is mentally prepared, it's time for the last and final step, understanding the information. This step leads me to the structure behind writing this book. When learning and understanding new information, my mind works very systematically. I am wired to wonder the who, what, where, why, and how of whatever I am learning.

For example, when I was a Firefighter/Paramedic, I was told to do certain things and complete certain tasks in a very specific way. I couldn't help but always ask WHY it had to be done that way. I was completely unsatisfied until I knew the reason for it. Being told "that's just the way it is" didn't cut it for me.

This concept of *Betting on Red* is not a book filled with a bunch of "pump you up" type of information that's oftentimes full of hype, extremely vague, and hard to apply. On the contrary, it is filled with life-changing concepts that are broken down using a step-by-step method so they can be easily applied and true peace, hope, and happiness radically discovered. We'll discuss where real peace comes from and how to fully experience it, while simultaneously weaving in short stories and analogies throughout to make it fun and interesting. This information was crafted using seven bible verses that could lead to an incredible transformation of your heart, mind, and soul in a matter of hours for all who crave it.

There is a lot of talk about peace these days and many philosophies have bombarded our culture. When I hear their ideas, they are drastically different from what I am about to share. Most spiritual beliefs have to do with being or doing all things religious to earn some points with God. Not here. I am talking about something far easier that guarantees victory. Sit back and relax while I uncover how to win the jackpot of a lifetime.

CHAPTER 1

THE PAINFUL BEGINNING

As we journey through life, we've all witnessed quite an interesting paradox. We've seen triumph come from tragedy, success from sadness and prosperity from pain. Some of life's most joy-filled moments actually only come to fruition because of a painful beginning. Take for example a mother about to give birth to her first child. After enduring excruciating pain during delivery, she finds that her distress quickly turns to pure joy as she holds her baby in her arms for the first time. Although tough to endure, pain will oftentimes awaken new life that never would've happened otherwise.

Such is the case with Doug Grimes, a young man who lived in a small town outside Nashville, Tennessee. He was an ordinary, good-looking twenty-three-year-old kid who seemed happy on the outside but was dying on the inside.

One particular Friday night would change his life forever. About seven o'clock, Doug and some of his friends went to a local sports bar for karaoke night. They were having a blast. After seemingly endless rounds of whiskey and karaoke, it was time to call it a night. They all parted ways and drove home.

Not one of his friends that night would have guessed Doug was battling for his life. Several years earlier, he had begun having shooting pain in his back and found himself growing more and more tired as the months went on. He would occasionally urinate blood, along with many other symptoms that he totally ignored. On his way home this particular night, the pain got the best of him.

Driving down the local Highway 40 about two in the morning, he suddenly clutched his side. The pain became so unbearable that he could hardly keep his eyes on the road. He drove toward home as fast as he could to get his parents to drive him to the hospital. As Doug reached down for his cell phone to let his parents know he was on the way, another wave of excruciating pain shot through his side and across his chest. He swerved his truck over to the side of the road to call 911.

As he swerved, the worst thing possible happened. A loud *thump* came from the front of his truck. Complete terror came over him as never before. Petrified, he thought, *What did I just hit? Oh my God, what do I do? What if I hit a person?* Panic and fear struck him to the point that he momentarily forgot all about the pain. In complete shock, he drove home as fast as he could.

He made it home and his parents drove him to the emergency room. After blood work and other tests, Doug learned he was in kidney failure. He had to get on the kidney transplant list and start dialysis treatment right away. His world had come crashing down and the good life as he knew it was over in a single night.

The next morning, his dad went home to grab some things for Doug to have at the hospital. As he approached the family van, he noticed a large dent and a headlight dangling from Doug's truck. The news report he had been listening to only moments before suddenly had new meaning. Reporters were telling a horrifying story of a homeless man found dead on the side of Highway 40, assumed to be struck by a car at a high rate of speed just a few miles from their home.

Fear and disbelief rolled through his dad's mind as he drove to the hospital. *What if my son did that? Could he just hit someone and take off?* Not knowing how to approach the conversation, he walked into the hospital room with a grief-stricken look all over his face. Noticing it immediately, Doug said, "Dad, I'm going to be okay. I'll get the transplant, and I'll be okay."

"Doug, did you hit something last night?"

Doug's heart sank to the floor. "Uh… I don't think so. Why?"

"Why is there a huge dent on the passenger side of your truck and your headlight all busted up?" His dad grabbed the hospital remote and turned on the TV. The local news had been covering the story nonstop since the morning broadcast. The caption read, "MAN-HUNT FOR HIT AND RUN DRIVER."

Not able to control himself, Doug yelled back at his dad out of guilt. "How could you possibly think your son could do such a thing!" At that moment, his dad knew that Doug was the one. He had always reacted like this when he was guilty of something.

Two months passed, and Doug still denied the whole incident. His dad's conscience got the best of him, and he reported his son to the police. That night Doug was picked up for questioning and later arrested. Still, he denied everything but had no answers for the damaged car, where he was that night, what road he was driving on…or anything else.

Several months more passed, and his case went to trial. The evidence had mounted against him. His attorney advised him to stay quiet and not to answer any questions unless he had to. The time had come, and the moment he feared most now became a reality; he was asked to take the stand. He now had to face the family of the homeless man he had killed.

Doug was heartbroken about what he had done. He took the difficult glance over at the homeless man's father to witness his head buried in his lap, crying his eyes out. Doug couldn't help it anymore. Suddenly, out of nowhere, he just screamed out, "I did it! I am so sorry. I did it!"

He admitted his guilt to everyone in the courtroom that day. Doug thought to himself, *I have only a few years to live. I want to live them the right way, even if I spend the rest of my life in jail.* He left the stand and got on his knees to beg forgiveness from the judge and the father of the homeless man.

Sobbing uncontrollably, he revealed the whole story to everyone in the courtroom. He started with the beginning of his pain several years before and ended the story when he felt the sharp pain and swerved over to the side of the road. Everyone in the room sat there shocked at what they were hearing. The judge was stunned by Doug's confession and was moved with compassion for him. He believed Doug was truly sorry and not just sorry he got caught.

The judge was also deeply moved for another reason. Doug looked very sick. The kidney failure was getting the best of him. His skin had a bluish-purple tint to it from the toxins in his body, making it obvious that he didn't have much time. Doug's insurance did not cover kidney dialysis treatment. While they were getting the insurance all sorted out, the hospital would give him dialysis only on an emergency basis.

Life has an interesting way of working out. Just days before this trial, the judge's son had come to his dad and told him about a recurring dream he was having. He was troubled that he couldn't get the images out of his head as they played over and over. Describing the dream to his dad, he said, "A bluish-purple man came to me and said, 'I am truly sorry. I want to change! I need your help! Please, if you don't help me, I am going to die. Please help!'"

The instant Doug admitted his guilt in the courtroom, the judge recalled the details of his son's dream. Astonished, the judge sat on the bench, realizing that he was staring at the "bluish-purple man" of his son's vision standing right in front of him. He knew something super-natural was happening and was conflicted about what to do next.

As he sat there processing it all, the judge felt it was still his duty to be just for the sake of the homeless man's family. To fulfill his responsibility as a judge, he had to render a judgment. However, rather than sentencing Doug to life in prison, he compassionately sentenced him to seven years in prison with a possibility of parole in two years.

The next day, the judge took his son to Doug's jail cell to meet him. The two had an amazing bond and felt as though they had been friends for years. After several hours of talking, his son had a strong desire to take blood tests to see if he would be a match for a kidney. No one wanted to set their hopes too high because the chances of this one random stranger being a match for Doug was slim to none.

Doug and the judge finally received the test results in the mail after a grueling month and a half wait. As they skimmed the letter, halfway down the bottom of the page read the lab results: "Identical Kidney Match." They all reflected the miraculous nature of this entire situation and knew this was destiny at work. The double surgery was scheduled right away.

The operation itself turned out to be a huge success. The hospital monitored the boys in the months following the surgery and both boys continued in good health. Their bond continued to get stronger as the years passed and their families grew close together as if they were one. The whole ordeal turned out to be a true modern-day miracle that inspired all the people that heard their story.

Doug didn't know the tremendous amount of hope that was waiting for him after he confessed his sins to the compassionate judge. If he would've kept running, he never would have discovered that the judge's son was ready and willing to risk his own life to save him. Admitting his sin was painful at first, but Doug's sorrow led to pure joy when he surrendered himself, only to find the hope that was waiting for him just around the corner.

Here we are at the first and most powerful step to the magic of betting on red that surpasses all human logic and understanding. We may not realize it, but by taking the painful step of admitting our sins, we can start on the road to victory that will satisfy the deepest part of our souls and allow us to experience an amazing life beyond our wildest dreams.

I want to begin to unfold the betting on red process with a special behind-the-scenes look at this issue of sin and where it came from. We will slowly unfold the love story of a compassionate Judge and his loving Son who will single-handedly destroy the negative impact of our sin, resulting in an overflowing amount of that mercy, peace, hope, and happiness we all hunger for. The beginning of this concept dates to the foundation of the world as we know it. Here we go.

The First Appearance of Sin

From the beginning of the universe, God created a wide variety of living creatures—from plants and trees to land and sea animals to flying creatures to microscopic organisms. From the hand of his creativity were fashioned beings designed to live with him forever in paradise: his army of angels and the human family they were designed to protect.

These mighty angels were breathtaking in appearance. One of the most attractive angels ever created was an angel named Lucifer, or "Light Bearer." We are told his wings covered the very throne of God himself. It is with Lucifer that our story begins.

God recounts the history of Lucifer in the book of Ezekiel:

> You were in Eden, the garden of God; every precious stone adorned you: carnelian, chrysolite and, emerald, topaz, onyx and jasper, lapis lazuli, turquoise, and beryl. Your settings and mountings were made of gold; on the day you were created they were prepared. You were anointed as a guardian cherub, for so I ordained you. You were on the holy mount of God; you walked among the fiery stones. You were blameless in your ways from the day you were created till wickedness was found in you. Through your widespread trade, you were filled with violence, and you sinned. So I drove you in disgrace from the mount of God, and I expelled you, guardian cherub, from among the fiery stones. Your heart became proud on account of your beauty, and you corrupted your wisdom because of your splendor. So I threw you to the earth; I made a spectacle of you before kings. By your many sins and dishonest trade, you have desecrated your sanctuaries. So I made a fire come out from you, and it consumed you, and I reduced you to ashes on the ground in the sight of all who were watching. (Ezekiel 28:13–18)

For the first time in history, sin was found—in Lucifer. Because of his gorgeous appearance, he became full of ego and pride. His jealousy and thirst for power mounted against the God who had created him. Other scriptures reveal that one-third of all God's angels followed him in the rebellion in an attempt to take over the throne. Instantaneously his name changed from Lucifer (Light Bearer) to Satan or Devil (Opposer).

The prophet Isaiah gives us more insight into the extent of Lucifer's ego.

> How you have fallen from heaven, morning star, son of the dawn! You have been cast down to the earth, you who once laid low the nations! You said in your heart, "I will ascend to the heavens; I will raise my throne above the stars of God; I will sit enthroned on the mount of assembly, on the utmost heights of Mount Zaphon. I will ascend above the tops of the clouds; I will make myself like the Most High." But you are brought down to the realm of the dead, to the depths of the pit. (Isaiah 14:12–15)

Satan forgot that he was a created being and that God was the one who made him so attractive. His sin caused him to lose his home in paradise, and he was "cast down to the earth."

What exactly is Satan doing on the earth? Job 2:2 tells us this:

> And the LORD said to Satan, "Where have you come from?"
>
> Satan answered the LORD, "From roaming throughout the earth, going back and forth on it."

Then Peter expanded more specifically:

> Your enemy the devil prowls around like a roaring lion looking for someone to devour. (1 Peter 5:8)

We witness Satan's collision course with humanity as he is roaming to and fro on the earth. It is here on this collision course that we come to the first of seven key verses and the beginning of the road to an everlasting peace that surpasses all understanding.

Verse 1

For all have sinned and fallen short of the glory of
God. (Romans 3:23)

Adam and Eve were living a dream life in God's earthly paradise of Eden. Life couldn't get any better. They took walks with God himself in the cool of the day and enjoyed the paradise created for them. They were free to enjoy the land and each other and do anything they wanted to with the exception of two simple commands.

I'll paraphrase these two simple rules: multiply yourselves by making love to each other and eat anything you want except for fruit from the tree in the midst of the garden. If you eat it, it will kill you. It was that simple. One rule was for pleasure and to carry on the human race and the other was given to protect God's children from death.

With these two commands, God gave an amazing gift, the gift of free will. God gave Adam and Eve the option to obey his two commands while also giving them the freedom to do whatever they wanted to do. As we'll see, God allowed a certain temptation in order to show that he wasn't going to force them to obey as a dictator would. Their voluntary obedience would prove they respected him spontaneously and their love for each other wasn't forced.

The originator of sin, Satan himself, was roaming one fateful day in the Earth's garden paradise. He had a simple agenda—destruction. His idea was to tempt Adam and Eve to break one of the two laws given to them. As long as they followed their father's instructions, they would not fail. Let's pick the story up in Genesis 3.

Now the serpent was more crafty than any of the
wild animals the LORD God had made. He said

to the woman, "Did God really say, 'You must not eat from any tree in the garden'?"

The woman said to the serpent, "We may eat fruit from the trees in the garden, but God did say, 'You must not eat fruit from the tree that is in the middle of the garden, and you must not touch it, or you will die.'"

"You will not certainly die," the serpent said to the woman. "For God knows that when you eat from it your eyes will be opened, and you will be like God, knowing good and evil." (Genesis 3:1–5)

Eve, knowing God's two rules could have exercised her free will to tell the serpent to pack his bags. Let's see what happened next.

When the woman saw that the fruit of the tree was good for food and pleasing to the eye, and also desirable for gaining wisdom, she took some and ate it. She also gave some to her husband, who was with her, and he ate it. Then the eyes of both of them were opened, and they realized they were naked; so they sewed fig leaves together and made coverings for themselves.

Then the man and his wife heard the sound of the LORD God as he was walking in the garden in the cool of the day, and they hid from the LORD God among the trees of the garden. But the LORD God called to the man, "Where are you?"

He answered, "I heard you in the garden, and I was afraid because I was naked; so I hid."

And he said, "Who told you that you were naked? Have you eaten from the tree that I commanded you not to eat from?"

The man said, "The woman you put here with me—she gave me some fruit from the tree, and I ate it."

Then the LORD God said to the woman, "What is this you have done?"

The woman said, "The serpent deceived me, and I ate." (Genesis 3:6–13)

I bet it was the highlight of God's day when he got to hang out with his kids as they strolled through the garden. Then one afternoon, a once confident, happy, and outgoing Adam and Eve didn't make the meeting with their father. For the first time ever, they were ashamed of their nakedness and decided to hide in the bushes when they heard their dad's call.

Clearly, they had always been naked but never felt embarrassed by it. The joy and freedom they were created to experience were transformed into a sense of sadness and guilt they were never supposed to feel. The impact of sin quickly escalated as shame shifted to blame. Adam refused to take responsibility and pointed his finger at his bride; then Eve turned, pointing her finger at the enemy.

The sin that had begun with Satan was now birthed into the human family. They would soon find out that shame and blame were only the beginning. Now the downward spiral of life would begin. All life's turmoil, heartache, pain, and death would now become a human reality—and it was unstoppable. God's command to resist the forbidden fruit was a protective command, but now he'd have to protect them in a physical sense.

God swiftly moved into safety mode. To protect them from even more harm, he had to keep them away from the second tree in the garden that would have more of a disastrous, permanent impact. Let's take a look.

> So the LORD God banished him from the Garden of Eden to work the ground from which he had been taken. After he drove the man out, he placed on the east side of the Garden of Eden cherubim and a flaming sword flashing back and forth to guard the way to the tree of life. (Genesis 3:23–25)

Throughout creation, God had revealed his wisdom and creativity by developing a wide array of fruit trees with a broad range of flavor options and health benefits. Above all, there stood one tree that bore a single type of fruit that rivaled no other, the fruit from the tree of life.

God tells us in several places that the fruit from this tree has miraculous effects on the human body. Our early ancestors were gifted with the fruit from this tree that was uniquely designed with natural properties that continually healed the body and protected it from the aging process and eventual death in order to live forever in a perfect body. Let's listen in on a conversation between God the Father and Jesus about this incident.

> And the LORD God said, "The man has now become like one of us, knowing good and evil. He must not be allowed to reach out his hand and take also from the tree of life and eat, and live forever."(Genesis 3:22)

Adam and Eve found themselves in quite a predicament. Let's call it *the tale of two fruits*. By eating the fruit, they journeyed down the road of independence from God by choosing for themselves what was good and evil; despite the promise that it would lead to death. What would happen if they were allowed to continue eating from the tree of life while the forbidden fruit enzymes ran through their bloodstream? They would be stuck in an aging body, separated from their father forever in shame. God wouldn't allow that.

As any loving father would do, he had to block them from more disastrous effects, love them from a distance, and implement a plan to win them back. Adam and Eve effectually bet on black, and only a bet on red could reverse the entire process.

One generation after another followed in their ancestors' footsteps, pursuing pleasure over peace, independence over joy, and heartache over happiness. It didn't take very long for the entire world to become wicked beyond measure. God waited patiently until he finally looked upon his creation with this conclusion:

> The LORD saw how great the wickedness of the
> human race had become on the earth, and that
> every inclination of the thoughts of the human
> heart was only evil all the time. (Genesis 6:5)

What had started as disobedience to one command quickly snowballed to widespread wickedness. It escalated so that everyone's actions were only evil, all the time. Eventually, God had no choice but to institute laws and commandments that were essential to keeping some sort of harmony in the midst of his creation.

God never intended his children to be inundated with hundreds of rules to break in order to sin. His original two commands were easy and pleasurable and were solely intended to keep peace in the land.

Just as he did for Adam and Eve, God speaks words to us today to keep us out of trouble. The enemy comes slithering up to us through the garden of television, radio, certain friendships, public opinion, and various other ways—casting doubt and twisting the words of God, enticing us in every way imaginable. As we all follow our human nature and fall into sin, we find ourselves in the same predicament as Adam and Eve: separated from our Father and included in his plan to win all of us back.

Before we go much further, I must say that understanding that we're all guilty of sin is the critical key that leads to winning the jackpot of our dreams as you'll soon see. There are some people out there that like to point our sins out in a mean spirited fashion, but the truth is that it was never intended to make us feel condemned or hated by God like some tend to portray it. In fact, you'll see that it's the exact opposite.

Understanding that we've all sinned is the start of the painful beginning that leads to pure joy, not to mention the key that unlocks the treasure that awaits us. Just as Doug discovered, this realization starts us on the road to ultimate peace and freedom and a life beyond our wildest dreams.

Knowing that there's a tremendous amount of joy waiting for us within this *sin* word, lets cast the awkwardness aside and uncover the hidden treasure behind this ugly word. Honestly speaking, I often break the rules and sometimes take great pleasure in doing so—we all do. We may not even think twice about it, but this is what God's Word calls sin.

If I were to write down every sin that I've committed, the list would be in the tens of thousands. I can't help but recall the moving car that I sideswiped driving down the highway and then promptly made a u-turn, stopped for a few seconds and sped away. I distinctly remember the money that I "borrowed" out of the cash register while working as a host at my local restaurant. This is all not to mention the day that I showed up to school completely drunk before Mr. White's history class, causing a huge scene and disrupting a class full of stressed-out students during finals week. There are many more I could add to this list—but let's say the grace and mercy of God never fails and is unquestionably relentless.

As all of us have practiced many times, sin is the act of breaking the laws that threaten the peace and harmony we were created to experience. It pertains to acts that are carried out mentally and physically, intentionally and unintentionally that cause unnecessary harm to ourselves and others.

In order to sin, we must have a command to break. What command? Any command that is given by our ultimate authority—God. Our early ancestors had just two easy commands to follow and many more were forced out over centuries of exploring the liberty of our free will to choose. Let's take a quick peek at some of the original commandments.

God commanded his people, "You shall have no other gods before me"(Exodus 20:3). A god is anything that is worshipped spiritually or takes priority over God in heaven in our lives. For centuries, we have worshipped thousands of gods. This reality is written into our history books in the study of our ancient culture.

Among the thousands of gods, there are three especially popular ones, which may be still worshipped today—although sometimes under a different name. Take the goddess Ashtaroth for example. She's was the goddess of sensuality and pleasure. This is exactly who I was unknowingly worshipping while on the hunt to find fulfilling joy in life. I pursued pleasure as a marathon runner thirsted for a drink of water after a long race. Chasing Ashtaroth was my attempt to fill the drought in my own soul, although it never satisfied. Those of us who are living for pleasure and constantly seeking its warm embrace as an escape to the world's loneliness could be climbing into bed with this hottie.

Then there was the ancient god Mammon, the god of prosperity and money. This is a tough one that most of us struggle with. We want to be successful, provide for our families, and have nice things. However, when that desire drives our very existence—the ancient god of Mammon may be on the throne. I can't tell you how many times I thought about having lots of money in my life, to the point that I was jealous of everyone who had more than I did.

Last, there is Moloch, the god of child sacrifice. In the ancient days, people used to place their baby children in a lit furnace lying in the open arms of a bronze statue to burn to death. They believed that satisfying Moloch would ensure financial prosperity for the family and future children. This may sound way out there, but how many of us have fought for success to the point that we had to sacrifice our family in the process? I would venture to say this is a reality for a lot of us, especially in America.

The commandments continue (see Exodus 20):

- "You shall not misuse the name of the Lord God." This would include saying, "God d—it" or "Jesus Christ" when we're upset. This may be one that we're all continually guilty of.
- "Remember the Sabbath day by keeping it holy." This is taking one day off every week to worship God, rest, and relax, without working at all.
- "Honor your father and mother." This would include yelling at them or disobeying them. It means doing what they say—when they say it—as long as it is wholesome and good. In later life, as they age, it means respecting and caring for them.
- "You shall not murder." Jesus says if we have hatred in our hearts toward another person, we've already committed murder in God's sight (1 John 3:15). If this is the case, I've personally murdered hundreds of people in the eyes of God.
- "You shall not commit adultery." Adultery includes having sex of any kind with anyone you're not married to. Matthew 5:28 says that even if you look at a woman (or a man) lustfully, adultery has already taken place in God's sight. I would venture to say that most of us are guilty of this one at one time or another.
- "You shall not steal." This is taking anything that docs not belong to you, at any time. I don't know anyone on earth who would be innocent here. I'd be willing to bet that we've all stolen at least a dollar from Uncle Sam on our taxes, at least a minute from our employers with long lunch breaks.
- "You shall not lie." This includes small white lies, creative truth-telling, stretching the truth, or not telling the whole truth.
- "You shall not covet." This is wishing you had your neighbor's possessions—another one that's almost impossible not to do as a human being.

Countless times I toyed with the idea of doing something I knew I shouldn't. The more the idea rolled around in my head, the more enticing and appealing it became, and I got sucked in and became guilty as I did the dirty deed from this list and many more.

How can any of us be innocent, especially in today's society? We have all downplayed the impact of sin—just as our ancestors did. We have cleverly come up with the phrases like "girls will be girls," "boys will be boys," "what happens here, stays here," "no harm in having a little fun," "no biggie, it won't kill you," "try it, you actually might like it," and "you can look but you can't touch."

One of the main keys to understanding this issue of sin is internalizing that when we fail in even one of God's commands, just one time, it causes all of us to miss the mark of *His* perfection. We may have tried our best to be good, but it's impossible to be perfect enough to stand in the presence of a holy God. James 2:10 says, "For the person who keeps all of the laws except one is as guilty as a person who has broken all of God's laws"(NLT).

I talked to a man several years ago who actually said that he's never sinned in his life and that only I was a sinner. Well, he was right about me, but 1 John 1:8 says that he had sinned too: "If we claim to be without sin, we deceive ourselves and the truth is not in us." It's impossible not to sin; it is in our very nature.

The great news is this is not the end of the story. Hang on tight as I slowly uncover how extremely gracious our God is and to what length he will go to rescue us, reunite us to himself, and flood our souls with his peace, hope, and happiness.

CHAPTER 2

SEPARATED

Verse 2

> Surely the arm of the Lord is not too short to
> save, nor his ear too dull to hear. But your iniqui-
> ties have separated you from your God; your sins
> have hidden his face from you so that he will not
> hear. (Isaiah 59:1–2)

The prophet Isaiah brings us to the second of seven life-changing
verses. He's saying that it's not that God is physically unable to hear
us, but it's simply that our sins have separated us from a relationship
with him. We saw this happen with Adam and Eve in their garden
home. They were experiencing a real peace, harmony, and closeness
with God right up to the time they chose their own freedom from
authority.

I can relate to Adam and Eve. I felt this separation without
knowing that's what it was. Subconsciously, I felt I was hiding from
truth as I pursued my own desires and threw caution to the wind.
God knew I would never be at peace that way, so he lovingly placed
something within me that felt like a missing puzzle piece in my life.
He knew I wouldn't be able to sit idle and do nothing about it. Just
as he'd probably planned, the void led me to give up and give in to
the lover of my soul.

This book is written to those out there who feel the same way. They feel lost in this world and want to know what real peace, joy, and freedom feel like. They want to feel complete from the inside out and know they can't be perfect in this messed up world we're living in. They're tired of betting on black and giving into things that never satisfy but only bankrupt further. I know from experience that true treasure can be found and victory can be won in an instant, regardless of our imperfect human performances.

To illustrate this separation, I'd like to share a quick story about Sharon and her teenage daughter, Cassie. The two had a great relationship. As any parent would, Sharon loved her little girl with unconditional love and wanted her to experience the best that life had to offer. Cassie loved her mom in return but didn't quite understand the depth of a parent's love.

The youngster was getting to an age where a battle raged in her teenage mind. She began to doubt and question everything that was good around her while exploring anything and everything she could get her hands on that made her feel good. Cassie felt lost in the world and wanted to find her place in it. She gravitated to a group of friends who felt as confused as she was and shared the same beliefs about authoritative people in their lives. Cassie consumed herself in dark, edgy music and all kinds of drugs and alcohol. She was growing more and more comfortable living the life of a rebel because she felt less restricted.

Cass was getting to a very emotional age and didn't want to listen to anyone. As the years went on, it got worse. She grew increasingly rebellious and did the opposite of almost everything that Sharon told her to do. As time went on, she began to feel that her mother was of no value to her—just someone who gave birth to her.

The further Cassie got away from her mother, the more inner turmoil and crisis consumed her. Uninvited thoughts flooded her young mind, and she began to blame her mom for everything. Despite Sharon's care, protection, and love, Cassie refused to listen or believe that her mom was only trying to keep her out of harm's way. She felt tired of feeling controlled and wanted freedom in her own way.

Sharon had no choice but to love her firstborn from a distance. The nights that she wasn't working, she'd follow Cassie to and from parties to make sure she got home safe. When she was at work, she hired private security guards to watch her daughter from afar. It was the worst experience she ever had to endure as a mom. Sharon longed to have a relationship with Cassie but kept getting shut out.

Cass turned sixteen and met a young guy who had lived a very troubled childhood and was also quite rebellious. He was seventeen and a savior in the eyes of the young girl. The two fell in love, and she ran away to live with him. Sharon had no idea where she was and did everything in her power to find her—to no avail.

Cassie continued to turn to anything that would help fill the void in her heart that could be filled only with the love of a mother. She tried to satisfy the feeling of emptiness with everything the world had to offer, but nothing would do the trick. Cassie had a deep sense of need for her mother, but never acted on it.

She was seventeen now, and her boyfriend had polluted her mind with so much garbage that she felt she didn't need a mother. In Cassie's mind, returning to her mom would bring more of a miserable, boring life. All her other runaway friends filled their conversation with constant lies about how horrible parents were and that they were totally clueless about life. Sharon waited for years, hoping the police would find her daughter and bring her back—but she seemed to be waiting in vain.

I'll show how this story ends in a while, but as you have likely figured out, Sharon symbolizes our Heavenly Father, who was and has always been there for us with open arms. Even in our rebellion, he watches out for us and longs for us to return. Cassie represents all God's children driven from him because of our own disobedience. The distance in the mother-daughter relationship symbolizes the separation from our Father as we look for fulfillment in a variety of pleasures and freedom from authority. We end up sailing away on the sea of life to be the captain of our own ship, only to reach a storm on a distant shore.

The boyfriend and the daughter's friends represent the world we live in and Satan himself, who impacts this world in the worst way possible. They constantly feed us lies about who our Father really is, make us doubt how much he truly loves us, and, in many cases, convinces us our Father doesn't even exist. Unfortunately, this separation from our Father tears his heart into a million pieces. He knows how destructive this separation is for us and will stop at nothing to get us back while there is still time.

We hear God reaching out to his kids in the garden following their sin against him.

> Then the man and his wife heard the sound of the Lord God as he was walking in the garden in the cool of the day, and they hid from the Lord God among the trees of the garden. But the Lord God called to the man, "Where are you?" (Genesis 3:8–9)

This leads us to the third of the seven verses.

Chapter 3

Till Death Do Us Part

Verse 3

For the wages of sin is death. (Romans 6:23a)

Up to this point, our sins have caused a separation between us and our Maker. This separation continues until our short time on earth is up. When we breathe our last breath, we're dealt the hand that is inevitable to us all: death. Biblically speaking, this is called the first death. The poisonous properties of the forbidden fruit will run its course through the genes of humanity, and we'll go through the aging process and eventually die.

What comes after the physical death of our natural body? For those who have decided to place their bets on black, the Bible specifically calls this next chapter of time the second death. This is a spiritual death or a "soul death," which means complete and permanent separation from God. This final phase of the life cycle is completely voluntary and easily reversed with a single bet on red. Revelations 2:11 says it this way:

> Whoever has ears, let them hear what the Spirit
> says to the churches. The one who is victorious
> will not be hurt at all by the second death.

The separation between us and God is against every fiber of his being. In fact, he'll continue protecting us, revealing himself to us, and chasing after us so he doesn't lose us—his prized possessions. In a few minutes, we'll begin to uncover how he single-handedly pulled off the ultimate rescue mission, giving us the winning strategy to win the inexpressible riches of true peace, hope, and happiness that he originally intended for us to enjoy.

Why is there a penalty for death and separation from God because of our sin? Some would think that God actually says, "You will die now and be banished forever in your sin, you heathen punk!" That couldn't be further from the truth, as we will see clearly in the next section. The reality is that this separation principle is displayed throughout nature and science in many ways. Allow me to explain with a few science experiments.

It's eleven o'clock at night and you're in bed with all the lights off. Someone walks into the room and flips on the light switch. A room once hidden in pure darkness is now beaming with bright light. What happened to that darkness? The light overpowered it and consumed the space. It's impossible for a space to be filled with supreme light and darkness at the same time.

Here's another one: Let's say you're in a science classroom and your professor hands you a tiny vial filled with germs and bacteria in a liquid solution. Then he cracks open a brand-new bottle of bleach and tells you to dump the container of germs inside the bleach bottle. What do you think would happen to the germs? The purity and strength of the bleach would overpower the germs, killing them instantly.

You may have seen our last example when you were growing up. When I was a kid, my friends and I would bring a magnifying glass outside on the weekends. We'd hold the magnifying glass up to the sun and focus a small beam of the sun's rays down onto some unsuspecting ants that were cruising down the sidewalk. A tiny fragment of the sun's power was magnified onto these poor ants, frying them instantly. The sun's mighty power was simply too strong for anything to survive under its incredible strength.

These simple experiments highlight the fact that two polar opposites like purity and impurity, light and darkness, strength and weakness cannot exist in the same space at the same time without the weaker of the two being consumed. It's a scientific impossibility physically and even spiritually. The darkness of our sins cannot survive in God's presence because of how holy, pure, and perfect he is—we would die in his presence.

We have an amazing, gracious, and loving God. We cannot, however, overlook the fact that our God is holy, perfect, and pure in every way. He is so pure that he told Moses, "You cannot see my face, for no one may see me and live" (Exodus 33:20). Sinful man cannot live before a holy, pure, and perfect God and survive without first being made clean.

Let us look at another encounter Moses had with God.

> "Do not come any closer," God said. "Take off your sandals, for the place where you are standing is holy ground." Then he said, "I am the God of your father, the God of Abraham, the God of Isaac and the God of Jacob." At this, Moses hid his face, because he was afraid to look at God. (Exodus 3:5–6)

The presence of God is so powerful that Moses could do nothing but hide his face. I also see here that although Moses was just a mere man riddled with sin and shortcomings, God allowed him to get as close as possible to communicate with him. Our God is so merciful that although our sins create separation and draw us away from him, he draws near to us. As long as we live, he will continue to reach out to us despite how far we've strayed from him.

In addition to being holy and pure, God is also the perfect gentleman. He gave us the free will to be ourselves and make our own life decisions. He'll never force us into submission as a dictator would. He simply invites us to have a relationship with him—inevitably leading to a heavenly afterlife, but he'll never force that upon us. In my opinion, the freedom of choice is one of the greatest gifts that we've ever received.

If we use our liberty to walk without God and place our bets on black, we're racking up debts that are far too expensive to pay from our own pocketbook. I'm suggesting a much better way. For those who are hungry and open for peace and the meaning of life, God is waiting in anticipation to offer a jackpot that will turn everything around. This bet on red will pay off every debt we owe and replace it with a gold mine that will come out of his own pocketbook. Now let's get into the good stuff, the place where true peace, hope, and happiness begin.

God's Checkbook Pays the Debt

The first part of the verse we've been talking about hasn't been all that exciting…

For the wages of sin is death… (Romans 6:23a)

However, the magic happens in the second part of that verse.

But the gift of God is eternal life through Jesus Christ our Lord. (Romans 6:23b)

This is where our gracious God steps in and single-handedly solves the problem that separates his kids from his presence. With one act of love, he creates the winning strategy that changed our broken world as we know it.

God created a path for us that covers up our current sinful condition and replaces it, not with just one gift, but with many. In his merciful, all-powerful, and majestic manner, God instituted a plan to pay off our debt in full—while simultaneously flooding our souls with an overflowing amount of treasure from the inside out. Let's begin to unfold this incredible story of *red*emption.

We all know this most popular Bible verse:

> For God so loved the world that he gave his one
> and only Son, that whoever believes in him shall
> not perish but have eternal life. (John 3:16)

God the Father gave us the gift of his Son. But why is this a gift? How is this a gift? How does it all work?

Most of us have probably heard the name of Jesus or said the name of Jesus countless times. It's easy to see why this name has had so much publicity in our world. His name shows up in church and during holidays like Thanksgiving, Christmas, and Easter. Many people find themselves saying his name ten times a day without realizing it when they are upset or frustrated. Instead of saying, "Oh Buddha" or "Oh Gandhi," Jesus Christ rolls off of the tongue.

Not only is this name repeated daily but the name of Jesus and anything associated with him is under extreme attack like no other. Lawsuits have been successful to get the Bible and prayer out of schools, the Ten Commandments off our government buildings, and some churches forced to lose the cross symbol off their buildings. How dare we have anything associated with Jesus in public sight without the uproar of people crying, "Separation of church and state!" Why is this? Because there is power in his name unlike any other.

Why is there so much power in his name? What is his significance? Let's put it all into perspective first with a little story that takes place on the East Coast of the United States. A Dad, his son, and his son's friend were about to take off on a fishing adventure that they all had been waiting for months to enjoy.

The dad would be the captain of the ship that late morning as they all set sail on their fishing voyage off the coast of Maine. It was a foggy but calm day on the water, everyone was excited and already having a great time just having a guys day out.

A couple of hours into their quest, storm clouds began to brew in the distance that wasn't visible through the fog when they first started. Not wanting to take any chances, dad immediately began to head back to the mainland. The fast-moving storm caused the waters to get increasingly violent within fifteen minutes of the first sign of storm clouds. Five more minutes passed and the increasing violent winds caused the waves to surge uncontrollably and begin tossing the little ten-foot boat around like a rag doll.

The boat's motor didn't stand a chance against the power of the raging sea. They were still several miles from shore when the waves threatened to tip the little boat over. A large wave came and nearly threw his son and his friend overboard into the sea below. Terror struck everyone on board because there were no life jackets and neither boy knew how to swim in this type of water.

Suddenly, the rush of a fifteen-foot wave smacked the side of the boat, and the dad reached out to grab the boys, one in each hand. The weight of the boys was just about to pull them all overboard. Dad's grasp of the boys' cold, wet hands made it impossible to stand his own ground on the boat. Knowing he had to hold onto the boat with one hand or he would be tossed over as well, he had to make the most difficult decision in his life. He had to let go of one of the boys, or all three would perish in the high seas. With his son in his right hand and his friend in his left hand, dad's tears streamed down his face as he let his son go into the unforgiving waters.

Within a few seconds, his little boy was swept fifty feet from the boat by the large swell. Helpless and lifeless, his dad looked on in horror as he saw his one and only son get sucked under by the sea's merciless undercurrent. He wailed in agony over the decision he had to make—but the outcome was irreversible.

Admittedly, I don't think I'd be able to do what the dad did on that fateful day. We all have to wonder why he would choose to give up his only son to save a friend of the family. Well, the story unfolds that the dad knew that his son had faith and trust in God. Unfortunately, he was equally sure that his son's friend did not. The boy and his family had no faith, as they had openly admitted many times.

The dad's faith was very strong, and he relied on the promises of God. He knew he would be reunited someday with his son forever. If he had chosen to save his son instead, there would be one more young man separated from God forever, and that would be too much for him to bear. He painfully realized that this decision was worth it in the long run because everybody would win, although the road would be tough.

The next day, the dad got together with the family of his friend in their living room. He told them the story of the tragedy. In tears and disbelief, they were amazed that he would sacrifice his own son to save the life of their precious little boy. Then he uttered these words, "I am devastated at what I had to do. I am still in disbelief and have not even begun to grieve over the loss of my son. More importantly, I would like to share something with you that makes it all worthwhile."

"What happened in the ocean with your son doesn't even compare with what was done for all of us two thousand years ago. God, our Father, did the exact same thing by letting his only Son march to his death. The difference is, instead of saving the life of his Son, his plan resulted in saving the lives of the entire human family. He painfully allowed his one and only Son to suffer death so we could have the opportunity to spend eternity with him. Despite my grief, I have been given peace that passes all understanding. I know beyond a shadow of a doubt that I will see my son again. You too can have this peace if you will receive it."

Right there in the living room, he talked with the family and explained the whole reason for Jesus. Everyone listening felt pure love coming from the dad who had just rescued their son from sure death. They saw that he not only believed what he was saying—he proved it. They felt the love, compassion, and presence of God exuding from his speech, and they all felt compelled to accept God's free gift and place their bets on red.

Where does this whole Jesus thing come into play in betting on red? How does it all work—and is it necessary? I will explain this and more, but let's get real for a second. God knows exactly what he is doing. He created the world as we know it in six days, complete with the sun, moon, stars, and planets for his creation to enjoy. He filled the atmosphere with oxygen to breathe, eyes to see, noses to smell, mouths to speak, and our hearts to beat. He knows what's best for his kids and doesn't do anything unnecessarily. Our all-knowing, all-powerful God felt it was necessary to create a plan to win us back into a relationship with him because we are worth more to him than anything he's ever created.

CHAPTER 4

LET'S TRADE PLACES

Verse 4

God made him who had no sin to be sin for us,
so that in him we might become the righteousness of God. (2 Corinthians 5:21)

Verse four is the most phenomenal part of God's plan for us and the very doorway to beginning to experience the peace many are so desperately seeking. Our God is not satisfied with the results sin has produced in us and he's downright disgusted with the idea of having his kids separated from him. In superhero fashion, we're about to witness our Dad move into swift action to rescue his kids. Not only will we get to see his rescue plan, but we'll also see him destroy the death, separation, and emptiness that loom over us—transforming them into a lasting peace, hope, and happiness… FOREVER.

What about the sin problem that separates us from him? Can God somehow override his law that demands death as the payment for sin and allow us to enter His presence in the sinful state we are in? The answer is yes…and no. Allow me to explain.

It is a spiritual impossibility for us to survive in the presence of our God in the sinful state we are in, so that's not an option. However, because of his abounding love for us, he created a work-around. Just as any loving father would do when his kids are in trouble, he has put together a rescue mission, while remaining true to his nature and character.

God has two main character traits that will help us understand why he would want to rescue us. He embodies a character of *justice* and *mercy* unique to him alone. Let's start with justice. Allow me to highlight this characteristic by asking a question: What would happen if a murderer was allowed to kill repeatedly in our neighborhood, and the police purposely ignored what was happening? I think everyone would be in a fit of rage if the cops looked the other way. Perhaps they'd be so angry that they would take justice into their own hands and kill the killer themselves to protect their families.

Justice is simply making something that is wrong, right, in order to live in peace and have order. For God to be perfect, he must be JUST. Because of his just nature, our sin cannot be ignored; it must be dealt with, and the penalty must be paid.

Earlier, we talked about a judge who had to give Doug a sentence for murder to vindicate the murder of the homeless man. Imagine if we were the father or mother of the homeless man who was killed. I believe that we would have been comforted to know that justice was served. That was the right thing for the judge to do even though it wasn't comfortable for Doug, the accidental murderer.

The next and more attractive characteristic to us is God's mercy. He alone exemplifies this trait better than any human being ever could. He could not be described accurately without considering his abounding mercy.

Having justice applied to us is not comfortable, except when that justice is combined with mercy. Consider the following scenario: Imagine you're driving home from work one day and are running late for a dinner date with some friends. As you come to the next intersection, the light turns yellow, a natural invitation to speed up and make it through the light at fifty miles an hour. Unfortunately, you don't quite make it in time and slam into the oncoming car that was trying to make a left turn in front of you. To add insult to injury, you realize there was an infant in the backseat of the car you hit.

The police show up at the scene a few minutes later. Through a series of miraculous events, the family you hit decides to convince the police officer not to cite you for the crime. Not only are they successful in convincing the officer, but out of a moment of thankfulness that everyone survived the accident, the family decides to pay for the damage to your car. You are probably the most relieved and thankful you've ever been in your life.

Realizing you escaped without punishment, you get on your knees and thank God. You are handed down what you don't deserve because of the family's mercy. Your car would most likely have been impounded, a huge fine assessed with an impending lawsuit coming your way, not to mention spending a night or two in jail. But mercy reigned and none of those things happened.

Well, God's mercy is a lot like this, only much better. Using this analogy, imagine not only getting off free and the damage to your car fixed at no charge, but you receive an email from the bank informing you that a significant amount of money had been deposited into your checking account. As a token of appreciation that his family was okay, the victim's rich uncle transferred a million dollars into your bank account as a gift to spend however you wanted.

Well, God is that rich uncle we've never had. If we allow God to rescue us and bet everything we have on red, we can expect to have our sins thrown into the bottom of the sea, never to be remembered again. As if that weren't enough, he instantaneously fills us with his unspeakable blessings of peace, joy, and happiness on earth, while looking forward to a future amazing home in heaven despite our sins against him.

From the beginning of time, God's intention has always been to enjoy, bless, and prosper his kids. Since he is all-knowing, he knew his children would fall into sin and separate themselves from his presence. However, because our gracious God is awesome, he put a rescue plan into motion from the beginning of time to save us from sin's destructive path. His amazing plan would free us from the penalty of our sins, replace it with radical peace, and unfold a plan to pay the price out of his own pocketbook. This plan was strictly voluntary and never to be forced upon anyone, but made available to anyone who wanted it.

Since it was our sin that caused a separation between us and God, the only solution was to deal with sin head-on. There are two phases to his plan, phase one beginning before Jesus walked the earth. This plan was the temporary fix that would lead to a permanent plan found in the bet on red. Let's quickly look at the first phase.

Prior to the life and ministry of Jesus on earth, the first phase was a temporary plan by a unique process called *atonement.* If you break up the word, it will make sense: "at-one-ment" or to be "as one with" again. This is a process that allows us to be cleansed of our sin so God's perfect presence can dwell with us again. These scriptures offer us an introduction to this principle.

> For the life of a creature is in the blood, and I have given it to you to make atonement for yourselves on the altar; it is the blood that makes atonement for one's life. (Leviticus 17:11)

> In fact, the law requires that nearly everything is cleansed with blood, and without the shedding of blood there is no forgiveness. (Hebrews 9:22)

You may be wondering how blood would cleanse us of our sins in order to be "at one" with God and have our peace restored. Well, our ways are not God's ways—surely, we wouldn't ever think of blood cleansing anything. Here in Hebrews, God is saying that it is *internal* cleansing, the clearing away of our sins, that deems us forgiven and clean in his sight as opposed to doing a bunch of good works in order to be clean outwardly. God explains to us that he will accept blood to cover sins, and nothing else.

We knew first from this passage in Leviticus that the life of a creature is in the blood. Had the medical professionals back in the 1800s studied this part of Scripture, they probably wouldn't have experimented with a procedure called "bloodletting." Back in the day, doctors and barbers were one in the same profession. While in the barber's chair, these doctor-barbers would literally drain blood out of the sick patient's arm and fill them with non-diseased blood in an attempt to make them better. Perhaps you've seen red-spiraled barber poles in front of haircut shops that simulate blood draining down an arm. Of course, this practice resulted in death for many.

God's Word tells us that the creature's life is in the blood, and now technology, science, and medicine have caught up to verify this fact. Technological advances have allowed us to confirm that hemoglobin inside red blood cells carries life-giving oxygen to the body. In the same way that blood symbolizes life, it also symbolizes death. Just as our bloodletting forefathers discovered, we can die if we don't have a healthy supply of blood in our system that's free of impurity and disease.

The life-giving blood that circulates in our blood vessels is riddled with a disease, and that disease is called sin. Physically and spiritually speaking, this disease leads to the death of all of us. The only way to be cleansed of this disease is to be cleansed with purified blood that is free of sin and impurities. Therein lies the beautiful solution.

Phase One

The first phase of God's plan to cleanse and restore the human family was very unique. God allowed a perfect animal—one without impurity, defect, or disease to be killed upon a wooden altar in the place of mankind because of their sins. In a great moment of *switcheroo*, God allowed the purity and perfection of the animal to transfer to man, and the sinfulness of man to be transferred to the animal—who died in their place. This was an amazing display of God's mercy and justice as he implemented a way for the consequences of our sin to be paid for—while sparing his beloved children.

This workaround in the system was good for anyone willing and humble enough to ask for forgiveness and turn to God with an open heart. The animal took the hit, while mankind reaped the benefit of peace with God once again.

Let's take a quick look at this workaround in action in one of the most popular chapters of the Bible—Israel's mass exodus out of Egypt. This example will not only display the animal's death on our behalf, but will give us an enormous clue into the second and final phase of his rescue plan—the bet on red. Let's watch how God used his supernatural power to free and restore peace to an entire nation, protecting them from a bloodthirsty king of Egypt.

The Beginning of Red

The nation of Israel has extreme popularity throughout history because they are the direct ancestors of Jesus himself. For years, God had promised them their own land that was rich and fertile—one flowing with milk and honey as a blessing because they were the descendants that would eventually birth the savior of mankind into the known world.

The Israelites found themselves inching closer and closer to the promised land. A severe famine had brought them down to Egypt for food in about 1800 BC. Unfortunately for them, it would be centuries until they were allowed to leave. Over time, the Israelite nation became so numerous, the Egyptians turned them into slaves for fear of a nationwide takeover of the Egyptian kingdom.

The nation of Israel was in severe anguish and cried out to God for relief. God heard their cries and raised up Moses to lead them out of Egypt and into their new promised land of Israel. With God's authority, Moses approached Pharaoh on many occasions to demand permission for the Israelites to leave Egypt. Pharaoh, the Hitler of sorts, grew increasingly resistant and even defiant toward Moses and God. After many plagues and judgments, Pharaoh's heart remained hard.

There was no other choice for the evil Pharaoh and the others who had whipped and taunted the Israelites; they would be forced to feel the pain and suffer the loss of their own firstborn. God would pass through in one night and strike down the firstborn in all the land. That is—unless they had the protection of the blood of the lamb.

We pick up this account in Exodus 12:1–13:

> The LORD said to Moses and Aaron in Egypt,
> "This month is to be for you the first month,

the first month of your year. Tell the whole community of Israel that on the tenth day of this month each man is to take a lamb for his family, one for each household. If any household is too small for a whole lamb, they must share one with their nearest neighbor, having taken into account the number of people there is. You are to determine the amount of lamb needed in accordance with what each person will eat. The animals you choose must be one year-old males without defect, and you may take them from the sheep or the goats. Take care of them until the fourteenth day of the month, when all the members of the community of Israel must slaughter them at twilight. Then they are to take some of the blood and put it on the sides and tops of the doorframes of the houses where they eat the lambs. That same night they are to eat the meat roasted over the fire, along with bitter herbs, and bread made without yeast. Do not eat the meat raw or boiled in water, but roast it over a fire—with the head, legs, and internal organs. Do not leave any of it till morning; if some is left till morning, you must burn it. This is how you are to eat it: with your cloak tucked into your belt, your sandals on your feet and your staff in your hand. Eat it in haste; it is the LORD's Passover.

"On that same night I will pass through Egypt and strike down every firstborn of both people and animals, and I will bring judgment on all the gods of Egypt. I am the LORD. The blood will be a sign for you on the houses where you are, and when I see the blood, I will pass over you. No destructive plague will touch you when I strike Egypt."

The Lord was patient with Pharaoh for centuries as they beat, tortured and enslaved the Jewish nation. God's patience for the tyrant leaders had run out, but his protective hand for his people came running in. God prescribed that the spotless, pure blood from a lamb to be spread around the doorposts of their homes. As the Lord came through the land to judge sin, he skipped right on by the homes that were covered with the blood because the penalty for sin had already been served upon that household. The homes that weren't covered in the blood of the lamb had to reap the consequences and pay the penalty of sin from their own bloodline.

Their fates had been switched. The lamb was held accountable for the Israelites sins and they all got away with a free pass to the promised land. God used this story of the lamb sacrifice to give us a preview of how we would be offered a permanent solution to our sin. This "pre-Jesus" system of animal sacrifice was only a temporary "covering" of sin. The more sins that people committed, the more animal sacrifices had to be made.

The Final Phase—The Bet on Red

God used this system as a picture of something much greater that would have a permanent effect and change the world forever. The prophet Jeremiah wrote to the world that God would soon make a new pact with his children. This plan would no longer be written on tablets of stone like the Ten Commandments, which were constantly broken and required animal sacrifices to temporarily restore righteousness. This new plan would be written on people's hearts, offering the complete and permanent forgiveness of sin once and for all. God said this through the prophet Jeremiah:

> For I will forgive their wickedness and will remember their sins no more. (Jeremiah 31:34)

How would God upgrade the old phase to roll out this permanent one? Well, the lambs' ability to cover sin was temporary because animals aren't human. The permanent solution to the forgiveness of sin and eternal peace with God would take an equal sacrifice to a man. The only one who would qualify had to be a human being without sin and perfect in every way.

There lies the tricky part. God would have to scour the earth to find a perfect human. Not only would he have to be perfect to be qualified, but he would need to be bold, loving, and brave enough to lay down his life for all of us. As he shed his blood for mankind, this man's perfection would transfer to us and our sins would transfer to him. He would pay the ultimate price of death on our behalf.

Well, this may sound problematic, because we've been discussing the fact that nobody is perfect and we have all fallen short of God's standard of righteousness. After all, who is perfect but God alone? Here lies the beautiful solution and the power behind betting on red. Knowing there was no other way, God made the decision that no father should ever have to make. He knew that the only solution would be to send his one and only Son down to the altar of the Earth to be a sacrifice for the entire human race.

The Son of God stepped down from his throne room in Heaven and stepped into the world that he created. His mission was simple; to be birthed into the family and spend the next thirty years, proving himself to be a suitable sacrifice in order to take our sins upon himself. Like the spotless, blameless lamb of the old system, God's Son would have to demonstrate his sinless and perfect nature to be qualified. He would have to be born as a man, raised a man, suffer as a man, tried, tested, and tempted…and do it all perfectly. Jesus Christ, fully God and fully man, pulled it off.

Jesus was never greedy, never hated, lusted, cheated, lied, stole, or wronged anyone in any way. He was faced with every temptation known to man but endured them all without even one sin. Hebrews 4:15 says it this way:

> For we do not have a high priest who is unable to empathize with our weaknesses, but we have one who has been tempted in every way, just as we are—yet he did not sin.

61

After proving himself to be the perfect sacrifice, the very blood that circulated throughout his veins became the antidote we needed to reverse the penalty of our sins and give us the winning formula to a jackpot of peace, hope, and happiness for all eternity. *It's none other than the color red...the all-powerful, all-sin—eliminating, perfect blood of Jesus Christ.* His blood, spilled for all mankind, purifies us from everything we've ever done or will do. His perfect blood allows us to be viewed as perfect in God's sight and to live forever in perfect harmony as God originally intended.

Not only did Jesus prove himself to be a worthy sacrifice with his sinless track record, his time on earth allowed him to fully experience how hard this life could be. Our God went through all the trials and temptations known to man, stirring up deep compassion for us and an understanding of what we're going through. He has become an even greater advocate for us who fully empathizes with our weaknesses. He backed up his love by stepping down into human history to walk in our shoes and bear our burdens.

What did life for Jesus look like? Being fully man, he knew what it was like to be hungry, thirsty, and tired while working long hours in the hot middle-eastern sun as a carpenter. He knew what it was like to get up long before sunrise, take care of his earthly parents, and go through all kinds of heartaches, hardships, distress, and pain as he endured the human experience.

Being fully God, he also amazed the community around him. He healed the sick, raised the dead, cleansed the leper, forgave the thief, the murderer, and the prostitute; loving all who struggled with a variety of ailments and weaknesses. He made the deaf hear and the blind see—showing endless mercy to everyone regardless of how sinful they were. He was the perfect picture of God in the flesh as he performed countless miracles; moved by love and compassion for his children that surrounded him.

Jesus willingly laid down his heavenly crown to put on a crown of thorns. He stepped down off his throne in heaven to be mocked, beaten, spat on, and ridiculed by the leaders on their thrones. He took off his heavenly robe to wear a robe that would be saturated with his own blood. Ultimately, he would be punished with the punishment we deserve and become sin for us so that in him we might become the righteousness of God (2 Corinthians 5:21).

Jesus was uniquely qualified as fully God and fully man. He alone had the authority to transfer his perfection to us and suffer the death penalty on our behalf so we could escape judgment. God's permanent rescue plan through the sacrifice of his Son allowed his standard of justice to be poured out on him, while the flow of mercy to be poured out upon us so we could be set free. What an amazing and loving God we serve.

The lambs used for sacrifices in the old system were born and raised for the main purpose of being a sacrifice for man; Jesus himself was no exception. Let's see what John the Baptist said about this as he saw Jesus coming in his direction one afternoon:

> This encounter took place in Bethany, an area east of the Jordan River, where John was baptizing. The next day John saw Jesus coming toward him and said, "Look! The Lamb of God who takes away the sin of the world! (John 1:28–29 NLT)

Jesus was known to all his disciples as the Lamb of God. Perhaps they really didn't understand why John the Baptist called him by that name and that Jesus was being prepared as the Lamb of God on our behalf. Only after Jesus was crucified and fulfilled his rescue mission did they finally realize why he was called by that name. Jesus's life, death, and sacrifice completed the final phase of God's great and glorious plan from the beginning of time.

The Lamb's Suffering

I highly doubt the lambs of the old system suffered very much. They were instantly killed and probably didn't feel any pain. With Jesus, it was entirely different. Our human lamb didn't spill his blood for the forgiveness of just one person, one family, or one nation—but for the entire human population. The penalty of death that is due to every person who has ever lived was cast on him all at once as he suffered unthinkable brutality.

How severe a price did Jesus pay? The prophet Isaiah explains it like this:

> Many people were shocked when they saw him;
> he was so disfigured that he hardly looked human.
> (Isaiah 52:14 GNT)

It's hard to imagine that Jesus was beaten to the extent that he hardly looked human. Let's look at a play by play to see what actually happened, starting with Matthew 27:26:

> But he had Jesus flogged and handed him over to
> be crucified.

It may be easy to look at the word *flogged* and think nothing of it. However, flogging was one of the worst and bloodiest forms of torture a human could endure. The Roman weapon of choice was a whip known as a flagellum. History shows that this was a leather stranded whip that had knifelike fragments of glass and metal tied inside the knots at the tip of the leather strands. When the whip made contact with human skin, the metal and glass tore through the flesh, leaving behind a wrangled mix of flesh, muscle and bone. Extreme pain and loss of blood often left the victim unconscious and, in some cases, dead. Roman torture had no limit to how many times someone could be flogged.

That was just the beginning.

> Then the governor's soldiers took Jesus into the
> Praetorium and gathered the whole company of
> soldiers around him. They stripped him and put
> a scarlet robe on him, and then twisted together
> a crown of thorns and set it on his head. They
> put a staff in his right hand. Then they knelt in
> front of him and mocked him. "Hail, king of

the Jews!" they said. They spit on him, and took
the staff and struck him on the head again and
again. After they had mocked him, they took off
the robe and put his own clothes on him. Then
they led him away to crucify him. (Matthew
27:27–31)

The torture continued with blows to the head. The already
beaten and bloodied Jesus was now struck in the head with staff over
and over. That might not sound too painful until you consider that
the soldiers placed a crown of thorns on his head while mocking him
as king. These thorns were said to have been one to two inches long.
A severe beating to the head would no doubt press these thorns into
Jesus's head, shredding his scalp. This is probably why Isaiah said he
would not even be recognized as a man.

By this time Jesus had lost so much blood that it was a miracle
he was able to walk. As a former paramedic, I've seen how people
could go into shock after taking a lesser beating. Not only was Jesus
compelled to keep going, but he shouldered the burden of carrying
his heavy cross to the place where he would take his last breath.

The path to the crucifixion site was known to be about seven
football fields long. Given that it was the time of the highly celebrated
Passover, the streets would have been filled with people screaming,
yelling, weeping, and watching Jesus march to his death.

The Roman soldiers, Jesus, and the crowd finally arrived at the
execution site, also known as the "Place of the Skull." They laid him
down, stretched his already beaten body on the cross and drove sev-
en-inch long metal spikes through his hands and feet. The body now
secured, they tilted the rugged beams into position. They pulled his
clothing off and gambled the items away to people watching, leaving
Jesus completely naked in shame. Some found it necessary at this
point to yell and mock him some more, saying, "He saved others; let
him save himself" (Matthew 27:42).

Despite the pain and blood loss, Jesus remained focused on his
mission even as he was pinned to the cross. First, he prayed for God
to forgive those who were murdering him. He said, "Father, forgive

them for they know not what they do" (Luke 23:34). That's amazing. If this had been me, I would probably have been cussing and spitting back at them. However, Jesus displayed the true nature of God by showing undeserved mercy and compassion to those who were taking his life.

Next, he focused on saving. Hanging to his right and left were two self-proclaimed criminals. One of them turned to Jesus and asked for mercy in the last few minutes of his life. His request for mercy was granted, and Jesus told him, "Today you will be with me in Paradise" (Luke 23:43). It's amazing to me that in his darkest hour, Jesus was there to receive the man, simply by asking for mercy—not having a single minute to earn it by good works.

All Jesus's suffering, heartache, and pain worked together to execute God's plan perfectly. Jesus was faithful until his very last breath. His final three words were "It is finished." The penalty of our sins was paid, the separation between God and man vanished, and the doors to peace with God were flung wide open.

Miraculous Evidence that God's Plan Worked

The Bible encourages us repeatedly that if we trust the plan of God and place our bets on the blood of Jesus, we will have an unthinkable peace that passes all understanding. This treasure is so valuable that I think it's necessary to quickly look at the single most powerful piece of evidence that shows that God's plan was effective and is worthy to place our trust in.

The Resurrection

The resurrection of Jesus Christ has changed the course of human history as we know it. It's one of the most cherished and highly celebrated events across the globe, even to this day—almost two thousand years later. Every Easter Sunday, countless families get together to celebrate what their Savior did: conquer death and raise himself back to life. Defeating death and rising from the dead are the hallmark signs that prove he was exactly who he said he was. Here's how it went down.

Here is the account of the first Easter Sunday:

> On the first day of the week, very early in the morning, the women took the spices they had prepared and went to the tomb. They found the stone rolled away from the tomb, but when they entered, they did not find the body of the Lord Jesus. While they were wondering about this, suddenly two men in clothes that gleamed like lightning stood beside them. In their fright, the women bowed down with their faces to the ground, but the men said to them, "Why do you look for the living among the dead? He is not here; he has risen! Remember how he told you, while he was still with you in Galilee: 'The Son of Man must be delivered over to the hands of sinners, be crucified and on the third day be raised again.'" Then they remembered his words.
>
> When they came back from the tomb, they told all these things to the Eleven and to all the others. It was Mary Magdalene, Joanna, Mary the mother of James, and the others with them who told this to the apostles. But they did not believe the women, because their words seemed to them like nonsense. Peter, however, got up and ran to the tomb. Bending over, he saw the strips of linen lying by themselves, and he went away, wondering to himself what had happened. (Luke 24:1–12)

Imagine witnessing the death and burial of your best friend with your own eyes. In the midst of your grief, a rumor surfaces that he's no longer in his casket but has risen from the dead. You and I would probably do what Peter did—run to see the gravesite for ourselves. Reaching the site, all Peter could see were his Master's grave clothes lying on the floor, as he gazed in wonder and amazement. I can't help but wonder what was going through his mind at that moment. Perhaps Peter stood there, thinking back at all times that his Lord told him that he would indeed die and rise from the dead.

Jesus would take his revelation a few steps further. Not only would he allow his friends to witness the empty tomb, see his grave clothes lying on the ground, experience the angelic visitor, but he went one step further by appearing to them a few times after his death. Let's look at one of these encounters with a disciple some have cleverly named Doubting Thomas.

> Now Thomas (also known as Didymus), one of the Twelve, was not with the disciples when Jesus came. So the other disciples told him, "We have seen the Lord!"
>
> But he said to them, "Unless I see the nail marks in his hands and put my finger where the nails were, and put my hand into his side, I will not believe."
>
> A week later his disciples were in the house again, and Thomas was with them. Though the doors were locked, Jesus came and stood among them and said, "Peace be with you!" Then he said to Thomas, "Put your finger here; see my hands. Reach out your hand and put it into my side. Stop doubting and believe."
>
> Thomas said to him, "My Lord and my God!"
>
> Then Jesus told him, "Because you have seen me, you have believed; blessed are those who have not seen and yet have believed." (John 20:24–29)

This is powerful. Thomas had to see the Lord and touch his wounds in order to believe. After all, he knew of his torture and certain death just days before. Realizing Jesus was truly alive, he confessed Jesus was his God. Jesus makes a point to say, "Blessed are those who have not seen and yet have believed." One translation for *blessed* is "happy." Happy are those who have not seen, yet still believe. What a treasure that is. This is proof from our Master's lips that betting on his blood gives us true happiness.

The natural human tendency is to say, "If I see, I will believe," but God's way is "If you believe, then you will see." Like Thomas, we too can put our trust in Jesus's resurrection and be filled with true happiness if we would simply believe.

Why is the resurrection so important? The apostle Paul explains its power and significance:

> But if it is preached that Christ has been raised from the dead, how can some of you say that there is no resurrection of the dead? If there is no resurrection of the dead, then not even Christ has been raised. And if Christ has not been raised, our preaching is useless and so is your faith. More than that, we are then found to be false witnesses about God, for we have testified about God that he raised Christ from the dead. But he did not raise him if in fact the dead are not raised. For if the dead are not raised, then Christ has not been raised either. And if Christ has not been raised, your faith is futile; you are still in your sins. (1 Corinthians 15:12–17)

Simply stated, the resurrection of Christ is the most important event in all Christianity to date. All the events of Jesus's life, suffering, and death are for nothing if he weren't raised from the dead. If he weren't raised from the dead, then he is still in the grave. If he is still in the grave, then he didn't conquer death. If he didn't conquer death, then neither will we, and we're still separated from him with a useless faith in Jesus.

However, because he did rise from the dead, he did conquer death, and because he conquered death, we will too! That's the best promise that can ever be given to us in this temporary life we're living. The worst news in human history is that the "wages of sin is death" (Romans 6:23), but it's also the *best* news because our perfect God died in our place. Since he was perfect, he carried no sin of his own with him at death. He voluntarily carried ours. He went through the pain to pay our debt, then resurrected back to where he belongs. Jesus, the Lamb of God, was perfect on our behalf to satisfy God's righteous requirement so you and I can hit the jackpot of peace, hope, happiness, and an amazing hope of heaven for eternity.

Power Over the Fear of Death

The death and resurrection of Jesus does one more powerful thing for us; it destroys even the *fear* of death.

> Since the children have flesh and blood, he too shared in their humanity so that by his death he might break the power of him who holds the power of death—that is, the devil and free those who all their lives were held in slavery by their fear of death. (Hebrews 2:14–15)

As humans, we have a fear of death that extends deep down to the core of our souls. Try to imagine what it would feel like to be on a plane that was hijacked by terrorists with no way of escaping. Or to hear from your doctor that you have a rapidly spreading cancer that's unstoppable, and you have only six months left to live. How about being the passenger in a car that's driving down a snowy, steep mountain road when the car brakes suddenly fail as you barrel uncontrollably toward the mountain's edge.

Those verses in Hebrews say we are slaves to the fear of death. Many of us are petrified of the thought of dying because we fear the unknown of what is on the other side of eternity. Well, those who rely solely on the blood of Christ are given an absolute assurance that there is nothing to fear. In fact, we not only have the confidence of eternal security, but we take that confidence with us everywhere. This confidence contributes to a strong sense of peace and security from knowing there's nothing but absolute paradise waiting for us on the other side.

God's finished work on the cross was proven by his appearances to many, recorded in scripture and documented by ancient Greek and Roman historians. It's proven through the lives of people all over the globe who, after putting their faith in Jesus, are filled with inexpressible and supernatural happiness. I've personally witnessed the transformation of many of my friends literally overnight after they've given their lives over to Jesus. God's power radiates through them like electricity as they begin to experience the power of God's deposit of lasting hope for the first time. It's time to find out how to place our bets on red.

CHAPTER 5

BETTING ON RED

Verse 5

If we confess our sins, He is faithful and just and
will forgive us our sins and purify us from all
unrighteousness. (1 John 1:9)

If you've ever played table games in Vegas or cards with your friends,
then you're already experienced at betting. Betting on red is no different. The first step towards a successful bet is perhaps the most exhila-
rating part—knowing there is a prize to be won. The prize that we're
awarded is the most invaluable gift available, a life full of peace, hope,
and happiness—topped off by an incredible eternity in Heaven that's
supplied by the one who created it all.

The next step to making a bet is the realization that your bet is
completely voluntary. In order to win, you must be the one to decide
to bet. In our case, we're pursuing a life full of purpose and peace,
which must be pursued by choice. In my opinion, no story does a
better job of putting the freedom of choice into perspective better
than the famous fable from the 1740s—*Beauty and the Beast*.

You may know the story. The Beast was a former prince who
had a love curse cast upon him because of the way he treated a seemingly old woman who approached the castle. The reversal of the curse
demanded that he love and be loved in return. One day, a beautiful

woman made her way into his castle and the Beast decided to hold her hostage. One thing led to another, and over time, they began to have feelings for each other.

One evening, the woman's father was in trouble. The Beast considered letting her go but feared the possibility that she would never come back and he would lose her forever. He could have forced her to stay in the castle in hopes that she would eventually fall in love with him. The interesting part of the curse was that their love needed to be authentic, mutual, and voluntary. Out of sheer love for the girl, the Beast cast his fear aside and allowed her to go and rescue her father.

The magic of the story unfolded as the girl came back, the two fell in love, and the curse was broken. Having the freedom to leave, had given her the option to come back out of her own freewill—a choice with great reward. She began to love the Beast after having the choice not to. This story had a real fairytale ending as their mutual love broke the curse and she became the most treasured princess in the land, forever enjoying her life in a gorgeous castle.

This story parallels the amazing opportunity we have with our God and King. He desires to share everything with us, his joy, peace, love, freedom, and *all* his riches—but graciously allows us to go out to the world, hoping we will come back to him out of our own free will. It's a liberating feeling to have the freedom of choice to honor and love him back—a choice with great reward. If we make that choice, it renders the sin curse broken and we become the most treasured royalty in his kingdom. We'll get to enjoy all of his promises, while living in a gorgeous mansion that he's been preparing for those that love him. We'll go more into that in a little while.

The next step towards making a winning bet is to understand that when the prize is won, it's completely free—*never* to be earned. Imagine walking up to a Vegas cashier and offering to wash the hotel dishes in exchange for winning the jackpot at the next roulette table. They would think we're crazy. No, the winning formula was given to us in our hotel nightstand, freely provided by the Maker.

The same is true with the bet on red. We can't earn our way into peace with God, and we can't do enough good deeds to be clean in his sight. Even our best works are often followed by stepping into another blunder or two. Some people live day to day thinking they are "pretty good" people overall, just like I used to. Thinking back, that was a very dangerous thought. While we may be generally good people by human standards, it's not by human standards we are judged.

Knowing that even one sin separates us from him, he was aggressive with the solution to do something about it—to the extent of giving his own life in exchange for our freedom. The great news is there's nothing we can do to make God favor us anymore, love us anymore, or accept us anymore. It's a huge relief to know we can rest in God's work and enjoy the victory he paid for.

Ok, we know there is a prize to be won, we're playing voluntarily, and that the prize can't be earned—let's move to the last stage of our bet. *All we need now are the willingness and the courage to do it without a shadow of a doubt.* Let's talk about how to willingly and effectively assure a solid bet.

We're sitting at the table ready and willing to go "all-in", without an ounce of doubt or fear in us. It's really easy from here; we simply open our hand, let go of the chips, and lay them down on the table. In our case, we open our hands to God, confess our sins, and lay down our lives to the ultimate forgiver, restorer, and lover of our soul.

Here is the funny thing about God: We can *never* out-give him. Everything we give him, including ourselves, he'll give back time and time again. Just like the gambler that was able to double his money with a simple bet, when we place our bets on red, God gives us back the new and improved version of ourselves—one that's overflowing with an excitement for life itself. His forgiveness rains down from heaven because of his great love for us that becomes tangible when we confess our sins and turn our lives over to him.

Real confession of sin is simple. It's a genuine prayer of surrendering our lives over completely to the God of mercy. It happens with the simple understanding that we've fallen short of the perfection necessary to stand before a holy God because our sins have caused a permanent separation from him. It embraces the fact that Jesus felt compelled to absorb the death penalty on our behalf because of his love for us. This act of love draws us nearer to him, and he draws even nearer to us with "conviction".

Conviction is God's presence within us, mercifully, but powerfully helping us to realize that we've sinned and need forgiveness. If we surrender to Him and admit our shortcomings, we can respond with confession to the lover of our souls. We're making the decision *to turn* away from the things that destroyed us, allowing him to step in and fill us with his presence that leads to pure joy. This is called *repentance*, which is literally translated "to turn." Acts 3:19 explains it this way:

> Repent, then, and turn to God, so that your sins
> may be wiped out, that times of refreshing may
> come from the Lord.

This turning or repenting is the trigger that allows the sacrifice of Jesus to apply to us personally. This activates God's plan, and we are forgiven of our sin instantaneously. At this point, God can unleash the times of refreshment that we've dreamed of and our souls desperately desire. He has a child to start raising, loving, and blessing. Now God is in partnership with us to lead us on an awesome journey to paradise.

When you think about it, the end of the verse that started this chapter is radical:

> If we confess our sins, he is faithful and just and
> will forgive us our sins and purify us from *ALL*
> unrighteousness. (1 John 1:9 [author's emphasis])

It's that simple—and nothing short of amazing. If we sat down and wrote a list of everything we have ever done to sin against God, family, friends, and the law, the pages would be many. When we repent and confess our sins, God simply wipes our slate clean from everything we have ever done—past, present, and future. We are now trusting in Christ's perfection and become as sinless as Jesus in God's eyes.

We get to see this idea of repentance demonstrated in the conclusion of our short story about Cassie and Sharon. Cassie ran away to fully experience what the world had to offer. She lived on the streets with her boyfriend and other runaways for years and believed all the lies that were fed to her.

Sharon hadn't heard from her daughter for weeks, weeks turned to months, and months turned to years. It was torturous to go that long without hearing from her child. For all she knew, Cassie was dead somewhere on the street; the return of her little girl was completely out of her hands. All she could do was worry, pray, and sit by the phone waiting for it to ring.

Little did her mom know, the tables began to turn in her little girl's heart. The sadness of being alone began to wear on her. All the great friends she had met on the street had abandoned her, and her boyfriend had run off with another girl. She got to fully experience the loneliness the world had to offer. She would lie in the alley and stare at the sky, wondering what her mom was up to. Her mind was flooded with all the great memories they shared, and she couldn't stop thinking about how much her mom had done for her.

Running from the peace she so desperately desired had left her exhausted, and enough was finally enough. Early one morning, Cassie got up from her makeshift tent in the alley and ran to the closest police station. She explained the whole story to the cops—who she was, where she had been, and how long she had been missing. The on-duty detective searched the missing person database and found that Sharon lived in the neighborhood only two miles away.

The cops drove her home, and she walked up the steps toward the door and rang the bell. Her mother opened the door and turned pale as a ghost. She couldn't believe she was staring at her precious little girl for the first time in years, still alive. Shouts of joy filled the entire neighborhood as they hugged each other for dear life with tears of joy running down their faces.

Cassie looked at her mother. "I am so sorry for running from you. I can't even imagine what I put you through. I'm so tired of running from you when all you have done was love and provide for me. I love you so much and want to listen to you now. Please forgive me."

"Of course, I forgive you," Sharon said. "Are you kidding? I've searched everywhere and cried myself to sleep for years. I would have given my own life to know that I would see you again." The sin and rebelliousness that separated the two were now a distant memory. Forgiveness was granted instantaneously as Cassie confessed her sins and came back to her mother.

So it is with our relationship with God. As we wandered through the alleys of life, he stood protecting us, providing for us, and pursuing us. In our case, however, he doesn't just sit at home waiting for the phone to ring or waiting for a knock on the door. He is the one actively searching for us—going house to house, knocking on the door of our hearts in hopes that we'll answer his call. He will never enter unwelcomed, so he patiently waits for an invitation to dine with us and lavish his love and forgiveness upon us for all of eternity.

Jesus says:

> "Here I am! I stand at the door and knock. If anyone hears my voice and opens the door, I will come in and eat with them, and they with me. To the one who is victorious, I will give the right to sit with me on my throne, just as I was victorious and sat down with my Father on his throne." (Revelation 3:20-21)

Placing Our Bet

If you are at the table of life and at the point where you want peace so much you can taste it, God is knocking on the door to your heart. Don't wait, open the door. Throw your chips in and give everything to the lover of your soul right now. The Bible says plainly that if you confess your sins, he is faithful and just to forgive your sins and cleanse you from all unrighteousness. If you say this prayer and truly mean it, he will meet you right where you're at and welcome you with open arms. If you're ready, pray after me:

Dear Lord,

Thank you for loving me and never giving up on me. Please forgive me of all my sins past, present and future. I've been living my own way and I want to change and give my life to you. I believe you died for me and rose from the dead to save me. Thank you in advance for hearing me, loving me and forgiving me. Lord, continue to bless me and help me live your way.

In Jesus name, amen.

If you prayed this prayer and truly meant it, CONGRATULATIONS! The God of heaven has heard you and forgiven you, and the Bible says that the angels of heaven are rejoicing over you right now. You are the recipient of the jackpot of a lifetime and an amazing inheritance in God's kingdom. You now get to explore your deposit guaranteeing your new inheritance and reap a small portion of what is to come in the future. Let's explore this amazing deposit and the very premise of this entire book—winning a life abounding with true peace, joy, hope, and happiness.

The Source of Peace and the Deposit Guaranteeing the Winning Bet on Red

The gambler at the beginning of this book was given a deposit, a portion of the winnings given by the maker of the roulette wheel that would prove his bet would win without a doubt. Our maker has given us a deposit that is far greater and way more permanent. Unlike a cash deposit that quickly disappears, we're given something that all the money in the world couldn't buy. Let's take a look at how the book of Ephesians puts it:

> And you also were included in Christ when you heard the message of truth, the gospel of your salvation. When you believed, you were marked in him with a seal, the promised Holy Spirit, who is a deposit guaranteeing our inheritance until the redemption of those who are God's possession— to the praise of his glory. (Ephesians 1:13–14)

Those of you who are reading this book and still wondering where the true peace, lasting hope, and real happiness come from— here it is. Our deposit is the Spirit of God himself living and breathing inside us. When his Spirit takes residence inside us, all his peace, hope, joy, freedom, and power come right along with him. We get to tap into his supernatural strength like a real-life superhero. When we place our bets on red and allow the supernatural power of God to live within our mortal body, he floods an eternal dose of peace upon us like a rush of living water. Let's look at these promises that are sure to take place.

> The Lord gives strength to his people; the Lord blesses his people with peace. (Psalm 29:11)

Our Father promises to pour out his supernatural peace upon us and bless us with his strength. This is a promise we can take to the bank!

> May the God of hope fill you with all joy and
> peace as you trust in him, so that you may over-
> flow with hope by the power of the Holy Spirit.
> (Romans 15:13)

The God of all hope floods over us with joy and peace that grow even stronger as we learn to trust in him. His Spirit living inside us results in a supernatural filling of hope that is so strong, we're literally overflowing with it.

> Peace I leave with you; my peace I give you. I
> do not give to you as the world gives. Do not
> let your hearts be troubled and do not be afraid.
> (John 14:27)

You've probably noticed that the world we live in can be rather cruel and the gifts we receive in this world rarely last. Not only are they short-lived, but they often come with strings attached or with an expectation of repayment. That is not the case with God. He gives us the gift of his peace that will last an eternity, has no strings attached, nor an expectation of repayment. His peace is so astounding that we can rest in it and never have to be afraid again.

> For God has not given us a spirit of fear, but
> of power and of love and of a sound mind.(2
> Timothy 1:7 NKJV)

It's very difficult to live in fear when you're living with his peace. God brings along free gifts of his power, love, and a sound mind when he lives within us.

> And the peace of God, which transcends all
> understanding, will guard your hearts and your
> minds in Christ Jesus. (Philippians 4:7)

Perhaps one of the most rewarding benefits of having God's Spirit living within us is that his peace surpasses our ability to understand. He floods into our soul and acts like a security guard to protect our hearts and minds. The more time we spend talking and listening to him, the more these gifts will intensify.

> Though you have not seen him, you love him; and even though you do not see him now, you believe in him and are filled with inexpressible and glorious joy, for you are receiving the end result of your faith, the salvation of your souls. (1 Peter 1:8–9)

First-century believers were blessed with the opportunity to be eyewitnesses of Jesus's life, teachings, and miracles. Although we haven't seen him face-to-face, he left us a part of himself as a gift that's even better. God's Spirit is alive and well on earth, empowering us and filling us with an inexpressible and glorious joy because we have put our trust in him even without seeing him face-to-face.

The prophet Nehemiah says this about our new found joy:

> Do not grieve, for the joy of the Lord is your strength. (Nehemiah 8:10)

Going through life's ups and downs is much easier when you have the hand of God walking with you side-by-side. His Spirit, also known as the Holy Spirit and Comforter; encourages, strengthens, and fills us with joy that gives us the strength to navigate through life's turbulent waters. Perhaps this supernatural joy is what people from all around the globe are searching for. There is no greater joy for me than to share this amazing news so that others can experience the same joy and strength that comes from our generous father.

It's a natural human tendency to think we have to fight all of life's battles and discover lasting peace, all in our own strength. This can be really exhausting and simply not the case. When invited, the

Holy Spirit flows through our hearts like a rushing river, leaving behind these amazing gifts for us to experience.

Courage for the Sake of Victory

If you didn't take the leap of faith and bet on red, take heart, because victory can still be yours. You may have noticed the following paragraph on page 74;

> "Ok, we know there is a prize to be won, we're playing voluntarily, and the prize cannot be earned; let's move to the last stage of our bet. *All we need now are the willingness and the courage to do it without a shadow of a doubt.*"

Perhaps if you didn't bet on red, it has something to do with doubt or fear like it initially did for me. Well, things that are unfamiliar often breed fear and doubt. The gambler at the beginning of this book that made such a huge bet on red was probably a little nervous to risk $77 million for fear of losing it all. However, he had the promise and proof necessary to push through the fear and double his money. Fear and doubt will take over if there is no consideration of what will be won in return.

I remember the moment right before I threw my chips on red that summer afternoon of 1997. You better believe fear and doubt were right there with me in an attempt to stop my victory before it started. It was hard to consider the joy, peace, and promise of heaven that awaited me for fear of losing out on all the temporary pleasures that had a death grip on my soul.

The more I thought about it, the more I realized that the very sins I held dear, were the very ones that caused countless tears. Instead of filling the void within, they only increased the pain that I lived in. When the buzz wore off and the pleasure didn't satisfy, the cloud of darkness grew thicker and any chance of peace fled further and further from my grasp. I've heard many times that the definition of insanity was doing the same thing over and over and expecting a different result. Enough was finally enough. I decided to end all the insanity, overcome the enemy's lies, and go all-in on red.

Right after laying my bet down on the table and immediately experiencing all the supernatural peace and joy that was promised to me, two things become blaringly obvious. The first thing was that the enemy himself was the very source of that fear and doubt. Similar to a magician that has perfected the art of distraction, the enemy lurked in the shadow of my mind to bring a hailstorm of distractive fear and doubt in the critical seconds before my bet on red in an attempt to shatter victory before it started.

The reason for the fear and doubt was simple—to paralyze. If the attack was strong enough, it would've stopped me from winning everything; luring me back into an environment that's comfortable, familiar, and "safe." This, of course, would've resulted in a life unchanged, lacking fulfillment, purpose, and victory.

The second thing that became obvious was that the enemy's whispers proved to be a bunch of crap! I've had *way more fun* and fulfillment in life now than I've ever had chasing the kind of pleasures that ripped me off. My only regret was not betting on red a little sooner in life so I could have fully experienced what real fun and joy felt like in the darkness of my high school years.

Fear and doubt weren't the only two tactics that were used to stop me from winning. The enemy came crashing in at the last second with one more lie out of desperation; *"Shawn, now you have to be a good person and do everything perfect, your gonna suck and you'll never be able to do it!"* Well, Satan was right, I do suck at being perfect. What he failed to consider was—I don't have to be. Jesus did that for me. Satan's lies always come up short, and he's the real loser in the end.

Unraveling the Lies for Victory Sake

Satan will whisper sweet nothings into our ear and tell us we have to be "good people", and that's just what they are—*nothing*s. The truth remains that we can never earn God's approval no matter what we do. His love for us is unconditional and our newfound relationship with him grows quite naturally. As with any close friend, the more time you spend talking to each other, the closer your relationship will grow. When we pray, we talk to him. When we read his Word, he talks to us. The more time we spend with him, the more we feel his love, joy, and peace. The more of that we experience, the more we desire to follow his ways. The more we follow his ways, the more our joy overflows. When we mess up, he's always there to forgive and pick us back up; continuing to fill us with his gifts regardless of our imperfect performance.

By giving ourselves to him, we don't lose out on anything this life has to offer. In fact, if we're willing to give our life to him, we double our money because he gives it right back with major upgrades. He knows every good desire we have in our hearts because he put them there. He can't wait to make them a reality if we lay ourselves down into his capable arms.

Jesus said this:

> Then Jesus said to his disciples, "Whoever wants to be my disciple must deny themselves and take up their cross and follow me. For whoever wants to save their life will lose it, **but whoever loses their life for me will find it.**" (Matthew 16:24–25)

I was truly "saving my own life" before my bet on red by living by my own standard, and I lost it in the process. However, when I "lost my life" by giving it away to him, he gave me back a far greater version—the version that I've always dreamed of. I ran across a short story a few years ago that I believe does a phenomenal job of highlighting this point.

The Tim Jones Story

This is a heroic story about a bold man of faith, Pastor Tim Jones of Salisbury, North Carolina. Tim was invited to a dinner fundraiser event in the fall of 2014. At the get-together, he found himself in a conversation with Don Herbert, a former professional wrestler. Within a few moments, Tim found that Don was in end-stage kidney failure and it became obvious that he would likely die very soon if he didn't get a kidney transplant.

Shortly after the fundraiser, Tim began praying and talking about the situation with his wife. Pastor Tim began to feel a strong desire to start the testing process to be Don's kidney donor and shared his heart with her one afternoon with these words: "I want to give Don a chance at life, and I want to give him hope." Well, it wouldn't be long before he would get that chance. His donor results came back positive. Tim was a perfect match.

Along with being a pastor and a potential hero, Tim was also a surgical technician. He understood the risk to this type of surgery, knowing full well that it could mean giving up his own life to save a complete stranger if the surgery didn't work out as planned. Halfway through the operation, the unexpected happened and the doctors found a problem. During the operation, the surgical team stumbled upon an aneurysm (a bulging section) in one of Tim's major blood vessels. The aneurism had gone undetected in all the pre-operative transplant tests. If the aneurysm ruptured, it meant sure death for the heroic pastor.

What had been intended to be a three-hour surgery, lasted six hours. Surgeons were able to detect and fix the aneurysm, snag his kidney, and successfully complete the transplant. If Tim hadn't been on the operating table for a completely unrelated reason, he likely would have been dead soon from the aneurism.

I am sure Tim had battled all the usual fearful thoughts before the surgery. *What if I lose everything? What if I die on the operating table? What if I lose the quality of life I'm used to...* and so on. He had pushed through the defeating thoughts, and his miracle happened when he decided to let go of safety, security, and control. The man who was willing to give up his own life, ended up saving it in the process—just like it did with Doug in the opening chapter.

After finding Tim's story online, I was able to connect with him on social media. We talked for a while and he shared his heart with me. I could feel the joy of the Lord through the phone all the way in North Carolina. I could also feel the pain. He is still dealing with some health challenges from his surgery but continues to fight on with purpose and passion. Please pray for Tim—that he would continue to fight and share his story for the encouragement of many.

The Life or Death Choice—The Most Important Reason for the Bet on Red

Tim's story displays the difficulty and triumph of making a life or death decision, no doubt the most important decision of his life. The decision to bet on red is no different. The primary theme of this book has been revealing the way to win true peace, hope, and happiness—and a successful bet on red will provide that and more. *However, this is not the most important reason for making the decision.*

The pursuit of peace and comfort is really important in this life, however, nothing could be more important than preparing for the next one. This is where the real long-term benefits of betting on red come in, and perhaps the most critical point to consider in this entire book.

The Crash—Want a Parachute?

God took a pretty intense stance by marching to his own death to save, protect, and bless us as his children. Why would he take such a drastic measure? Motivated by his great love for us, he moved into swift action to protect us from an afterlife where we would be permanently separated from him. Consider the following scenario that helps to highlight this point.

Suppose you've boarded a flight from Miami to Italy on a jumbo jet. The plane comes to a cruising altitude of about 35,000 feet when you hear some commotion between the captain and the flight attendant near the cockpit. The conversation goes something like this: "Terry, we've ruptured our fuel tank and we have only twenty-five minutes of fuel left. We're about two hours to the closest runway. There is no doubt—we are going to crash. There is an escape hatch for people to jump and a parachute vest for everyone. Pass them out and prepare the passengers to use them. NOW GET GOING!"

The shy, well-meaning flight attendant comes out to the passengers and says, "I have a parachute here for each of you. Who would like to wear one? They're stylish, comfortable, and they'll make you feel safe if something were to happen to the plane."

People look at her as if she's lost it. Some respond, "What the heck, it can't hurt." After about ten minutes, the people who agreed to wear them realize they aren't comfortable at all and definitely do not look stylish. Surrounding passengers begin to laugh at them for wearing the parachute vests, so they take them off.

Most of the passengers start to notice the plane dropping rather quickly but don't realize they are minutes from their death. Suddenly, the pilot realizes the fuel is leaking faster than he thought and both engines began to shut down. In a panic, he tries to pull the nose of the plane upward in hopes of a successful crash landing in the Atlantic. He thinks he has a few more minutes to try another maneuver, but he is wrong. Without even a second for people to put the parachutes on, the plane crashes violently into the sea below, killing everyone on board.

This scenario may resemble how some of us have heard about the necessity of Jesus and his sacrifice. Some may have heard, "Give Jesus a try. You'll have a great time, and it's a pretty cool experience." Some people will do just that, give him a *try*. The reality is that it's not always a party, and Christians don't have fun all the time. When persecution or trouble comes around, or they start making a ton of money, or when people make fun of them for their new relationship with God, they say, "What a crock. I got what I needed—thanks," and they can't run away from the faith fast enough.

We may be tempted to tell unbelievers, "Come to Jesus if you want to have a good life." That's when they look at their boat, their job, their cars, and their great family and say, "I'm just fine. Thanks, but no thanks." But if we love them, we need to tell them the good, the bad, and the ugly. They need to know what will not only give them hope, peace, and happiness in this life, but more importantly to help them escape an eternity separated from God that's irreversible.

Consider an alternative presentation of the crash by the flight attendant on the plane. She immediately returns from the cockpit and says, "Ladies and gentlemen, we have a leak in our gas tank and have about twenty-five minutes of fuel left. At this point, we are too far away in either direction to land. We are going to line up and jump out of the back escape hatch and jump safely into the water. The captain has radioed, and help is on the way. Who wants a parachute?"

Suddenly, most of the people don't care how stylish or comfortable they are; at this point, the parachute is a necessity to survive. But some still do not believe the flight attendant and decide to wait and see what happens. The passengers who jump out with a parachute land safely and find a rescue boat waiting. Those who thought the flight attendant was crazy and didn't wear their vests ran out of time and fell into the sea below. The passengers had been given all the information necessary to make an educated decision. Those who took thoughtful consideration to the warning survived, while the others perished in high seas.

Jesus, God in the flesh, walked this earth and spent years teaching the good, the bad, and the ugly so we can live this life victoriously. His job on earth was not only to teach us how to have peace on earth but more importantly to prepare us for the next life—where our bets matter the most. He taught us that one day our lives would come to an end, and we would need a parachute to survive the landing on the other side. Jesus offered himself up to be our parachute through his death and resurrection, making the forgiveness of our sins possible.

Although the road to peace, hope, and happiness is wide open for everyone, many will choose not to wear the parachute provided to them. Just like the captain who thought he had more fuel left in his tanks, we do not know how many days we have left on earth. While we may have many, today could be our last. With the next two verses, we will take a deeper look into the intriguing concept of the afterlife and further explore the two roads we have to choose from. To party, or not to party—that is the question.

CHAPTER 6

WHICH PATH LEADS TO THE PARTY?

Verse 6

Enter through the narrow gate. For wide is the gate and broad is the road that leads to destruction, and many enter through it. But small is the gate and narrow the road that leads to life, and only a few find it. (Matthew 7:13–14)

The idea of a small and narrow gate leading to life may seem too restrictive to some. The human mind naturally begins to think, *there have always been multiple ways to get something done or to get to any destination.*

This way of thinking has led to many businesses, industries, inventions, and is the basis of entrepreneurship as we know it. Human innovation has transformed society. Mobility has improved from riding on horseback, to carriage rides, then to cars and planes. Communication has evolved from face-to-face and telegraph, to home telephones, then to bulky cell phones that led to smartphones. This is all because there are better and faster ways to do things.

But when it comes to God, this can't be the case. He's not like the human race that improves their plan as technology gets better, or changes course as more information becomes available. He is the

Creator of the universe and knows everything that is going to happen, long before it happens. God doesn't mess around when it comes to you and me, His chosen prize. He focused on the issue that caused our separation; immediately putting a plan into motion that reversed the damage so that we could live together in paradise forever.

If there were another way to have peace and eternal life, God would have said, "All roads lead to me" or "There is more than one road that leads to me." Instead, Jesus himself said this:

> I am the way, the truth, and the life. No one comes to the Father except through me. (John 14:6)

God allowed his Son to suffer torture because there was no other way. In fact, in the last moments of his life, Jesus asked the Father if there was another way, but he was assured there wasn't. During the last few minutes of his life, Jesus made his final plea:

> Father, if you are willing, take this cup of suffering from me; yet I want your will to be done, not mine. (Luke 22:42 NLT)

Jesus never got a response. He came to this earth to be our sacrifice and he was resolved to stay focused. He knew the road would be difficult, but in the end, he would get you and me; the prize that he felt was worth suffering for.

While the road to eternal life and ultimate peace is wide open for all to enter, many refuse it as the only way, which makes it the narrow road. Many will exercise their free will to choose and try a broader; seemingly less restrictive road. This road is very similar to the one taken by the crashing plane passengers that didn't want the restriction of wearing their life safety vests moments before their crash.

In a typical story-like style, Jesus compares the invitation to heaven, using the analogy of an invitation to a wedding party. As we'll see, some accepted the invitation, some rejected the offer and a certain man tried to "slip in" using another wide gate and broad road to get there.

Accepting the Party Invitation—Dressing for the Occasion

> Jesus spoke to them again in parables, saying: "The kingdom of heaven is like a king who prepared a wedding banquet for his son. He sent his servants to those who had been invited to the banquet to tell them to come, but they refused to come.
>
> "Then he sent some more servants and said, 'Tell those who have been invited that I have prepared my dinner: My oxen and fattened cattle have been butchered, and everything is ready. Come to the wedding banquet.'
>
> "But they paid no attention and went off—one to his field, another to his business. The rest seized his servants, mistreated them and killed them. The king was enraged. He sent his army and destroyed those murderers and burned their city.
>
> "Then he said to his servants, 'The wedding banquet is ready, but those I invited did not deserve to come. So go to the street corners and invite to the banquet anyone you find.' So the servants went out into the streets and gathered all the people they could find, *the bad as well as the good*, and the wedding hall was filled with guests.
>
> "But when the king came in to see the guests, he noticed a man there who was not wearing wedding clothes. He asked, 'How did you get in here

without wedding clothes, friend?' The man was speechless.

"Then the king told the attendants, 'Tie him hand and foot, and throw him outside, into the darkness, where there will be weeping and gnashing of teeth.'

"For many are invited, but few are chosen [have chosen to respond]." (Matthew 22:1–14)

God's intention for us is easy to see if we analyze this story. Heaven is compared to a wedding party that he prepared for his Son and his guests (that's us). The invitation to the kick-off celebration was sent out, but those he invited first refused the invite. Despite their refusal, we see God's heart in the next sentence: "Then he sent some more servants and said, 'Tell those who have been invited that I have prepared my dinner: My oxen and fattened cattle have been butchered, and everything is ready. Come to the wedding banquet.'"

God desires a relationship with us to the point that he refused to take no for an answer. He sent even more servants to entice his guests by offering the finest meal imaginable. Let's think about this for a second. That would be similar to me having to beg people to come to my house to sit back and enjoy a lifetime supply of all-you-can-eat, mouth-watering juicy steak; succulent seafood; or your choice of favorite food, topped off with endless decadent dessert—everything cooked and seasoned to perfection. It makes no sense to refuse something like that; nor does it make sense to refuse the invitation to heaven. Despite the enticement, many will refuse his offer. Jesus tells us, "But they paid no attention and went off—one to his field, another to his business."

Some have not only refused his message but also have taken it one drastic step further: "The rest seized his servants, mistreated them and killed them." Throughout history, we have seen prophets, bible teachers, and evangelists killed by evil men and jealous religious leaders for trying to spread the good news of hope to the known world.

After constant pleading, God will move on. Salvation through the blood of Jesus came first to the Jewish nation because that was his lineage and the geographical area he was living in at the time. When his own people rejected him, the message quickly spread to the surrounding non-Jewish nations.

The message moved swiftly to the streets: "The wedding banquet is ready, but those I invited did not deserve to come. So go to the street corners and invite to the banquet anyone you find." God's message spread to anyone who would hear, and then "the wedding hall was filled with guests." Heaven will be filled with guests, yet there will be some that try to crash the party.

Jesus points out that someone tried to "slip in" to the party uninvited without their wedding clothes on… Jesus continued, "But when the king came in to see the guests, he noticed a man there who was not wearing wedding clothes. He asked, 'How did you get in here without wedding clothes, friend?' The man was speechless."

The point that he's making here is that there's no "back road" or "alternate route" to get into the party, although it seems to be a popular belief. Entrance is freely given to those who have their wedding clothes on. What are our wedding clothes? Let's look at how the prophet Isaiah explained it:

> I delight greatly in the Lord; my soul rejoices in my God. For he has clothed me with garments of salvation and arrayed me in a robe of his righteousness, as a bridegroom adorns his head like a priest, and as a bride adorns herself with her jewels. (Isaiah 61:10)

The banquet party is heaven and the wedding clothes we wear are garments of salvation; more specifically, a "robe" of *His* righteousness. God prepared a way for us to "wear" his Sons righteousness, giving us access to the heavenly wedding party of a lifetime regardless of our sins. It's that simple—nothing less and nothing more.

The Widest Lane of the Broad Road

When this man was spotted at the wedding party unprepared for the occasion, he was kicked out of the party and thrown out into the darkness where he would be crying and gritting his teeth. He was obviously trying to walk down the broad road and enter through the wide gate to get there; as Jesus said, *For wide is the gate and broad is the road that leads to destruction, and many enter through it...*".

As this man found out, the broad road was trusting in something other than the righteousness of Jesus. As was the case for me, he was most likely trusting in his own deeds. I concocted a belief system that I was a good person overall, which led to a dead-end and a God-sized gap that pulsated within my chest. Many of us look for a spiritual belief system that aligns with our own feelings and we unknowingly place our bets on black. There are many lanes out there on the broad road, but I want to share what I consider to be one of the widest lanes.

There are many spiritual belief systems and philosophies that teach works-based righteousness and therefore included in the broad road. Perhaps *alternate religious belief* is one of the widest lanes of this broad road. Have you ever heard someone ask, "What about all those other religions out there?" There is no doubt that on the surface, this sounds like a good question. However, if sin is the ultimate separator between God and man, what other religion has a solution to remove sin in order for us to be reunited with God in heaven? There aren't any.

There are many different religions out there, so I won't go through each one. An entire book could be written on this topic alone. Most people are concerned with picking the right one so they will be safe in the afterlife. In my opinion, all the world's religions and philosophies can be easily summed up in two views by asking one simple question: What do you have to DO to find peace and get to heaven?

The First View

The first view is a works-oriented view. This category includes every philosophy and religion under the sun. This is a belief that getting into heaven is somehow based upon how good they were, how many good things they've done, or how good of a mental state they've achieved. This belief is shared not only by religious groups but also by many non-religious ones as well. Some would say, "I have been a pretty good person; I haven't killed anyone" or "I have been good to people" and so on.

Some religious groups may say that you must do a certain thing or number of things to earn a place behind the pearly gates. The blessing of heaven would somehow be reserved for people who earned it in some way or another. This mindset is contradictory to what we see in God's Word. Isaiah says it this way;

> All of us have become like one who is unclean, and all our righteous acts are like filthy rags; we all shrivel up like a leaf, and like the wind, our sins sweep us away. (Isaiah 64:6)

As humans, we often think we're pleasing God by doing good deeds like being nice to people, helping the homeless, giving to charity, being a good citizen, being active in a church, and being a good person in a variety of ways. While these things are good things to do, we shouldn't mistake them for the perfection necessary to stand before a Holy God. This is precisely why God sent Jesus to live the perfect life that we couldn't live and give his life as payment for our freedom. Ephesians says it this way;

> For it is by grace you have been saved, through faith—and this[salvation] is not from yourselves, it is a gift of God—not by works so that no one can boast. (Ephesians 2:8–9 Authors emphasis)

We are created to have fellowship with Him and do good works for him out of appreciation of his love, not to be right with him.

Three weeks before his passing, Mahatma Gandhi confessed that he was in a swamp of despair and in total depression. This was a very good man whom people looked up to, but the very faith he represented seemed to leave him dry when it really mattered—at the end of his life. The truth is that anyone can create a religion and build a group of followers. However, having followers doesn't make it right. I can start a religion tomorrow and say that God himself or an angel showed me this was the right way. How could anyone refute me? It is not enough for someone to make a spiritual claim and then have a group of followers as the only evidence to back it up.

Any modified version of God's original, simple message of peace for the people he loves is not tolerated. Our God is a jealous God, and he is jealous for us. He loves his creation with a passion and hates deception that leads us astray to a different message. God originally intended to win us back with his own blood, not to be fooled into thinking that we can earn it by our own sweat and blood. We are too precious to him, and the price of winning us back was too great to allow any deviation of the simple message of faith in Christ and his righteousness.

The Second View

We have covered the second view quite extensively within the first one. Instead of asking what we have to DO to get to heaven, we should say, "All I have to do to get to heaven has already been DONE." Christianity is the only religion that says the work to get to heaven has already been completed for us in the life and death of Jesus himself. The price and penalty for sin is paid, and we are set free if we confess our sins and repent. It's that simple.

Christianity is the only belief system that includes total and complete forgiveness of all our sins—past, present, and future. The Creator of the universe holds out his powerful hand ready to flood down a peace that surpasses all human logic and understanding. No other religion in the world teaches that God loves you, is with you, and wants to help you through life's journey, backing it up by offering himself up for the cause.

Hell and the Silver Bullet

What kind of destruction does that broad road lead to? What does an eternity separate from God look like? Well, the answer lies in a single silver bullet fired many years ago. Let's resume our discussion of Lucifer to find our answer. Because of his beauty and splendor, Lucifer became an absolute egomaniac. His jealousy toward God and his passion to be worshipped consumed him, and he became the first of God's created beings to sin.

Lucifer was the first to be separated from God's presence forever. His sin caused him to be shot down to the earth as if a silver bullet had gone right through his chest. The bullet of sin knocked him off the road of heaven he had been destined for.

One-third of all God's angels were stupid enough to follow Lucifer's big idea of taking over God's throne. They too were hit by the silver bullet, sent away from the presence of God, and given an eternal prison sentence for their hatred and rebellion. This prison is what is commonly known as *hell*. Jesus himself declared why hell was created:

> Then he will say to those on his left, "Depart from me, you who are cursed, into the eternal fire prepared for the devil and his angels." (Matthew 25:41)

When the presence of God is around, there is love, peace, hope, joy, goodness, and ultimately paradise because his presence is the very source of everything that is good. When there is separation from God, then the exact opposite appears by default. Satan will be cast into an afterlife in the absence of his Spirit; inevitably leading to an eternal experience of loneliness, regret, and pain instead of the paradise he was destined for.

Hell and the Stray Bullet

Satan and his demons were hit by that bullet that cast them into their hellish resting place. Unfortunately, they were not the only ones to sin. That silver bullet was fired through their chests and kept traveling down the road. Which road? The broad road that leads to destruction that we were warned to stay off of. Hell was never a part of God's plan for mankind. When man used his freewill to sin, he began walking along the same broad road, with the same unfortunate destiny as Satan against every fiber of God's will.

This is what makes the good news, so great. God knew that drastic consequences called for drastic measures. He sent Jesus to the earth on a rescue mission to stand in front of us and take the bullet's impact on our behalf. His Son experienced hell, death, and separation from God for a brief moment—to stand in our place so we wouldn't have to ever experience what Satan will. This was why Jesus was so unwavering in his mission to be our sacrifice and absorb the death penalty for us. He died for the chance to be the hero of our souls that shields us from the stray bullet that's traveling down the broad road of sin and takes us safely to paradise.

God's desire for mankind is that we all are saved from the coming destruction and that nobody would perish. Peter said it this way:

> The Lord is not slow in keeping his promise, as
> some understand slowness. Instead, he is patient
> with you, not wanting anyone to perish, but
> everyone to come to repentance.(2 Peter 3:9)

The good news is that there is no place in hell for people who put their faith in Jesus and we will never perish. Although we will face problems in this life on earth, we do not face them alone. We have nothing but God's saving hand of protection, and our own place in heaven which we're getting to in a few moments.

The Rich Man and His Journey to the Other Side

If we had the opportunity to sit down and have a conversation with God himself to ask him what hell is like, what would he say? How would he describe it? Well, we're in luck because Jesus described it for us through the story of Lazarus and the rich man.

Jesus often spent hours with people teaching on a variety of subjects. One day Jesus was invited to dinner at the home of a prominent religious ruler. Jesus began to share a story with the crowd about a rich man whose life led him down the broad road. Let's listen in.

> There was a rich man who was dressed in purple and fine linen and lived in luxury every day. At his gate was laid a beggar named Lazarus, covered with sores and longing to eat what fell from the rich man's table. Even the dogs came and licked his sores.
>
> The time came when the beggar died and the angels carried him to Abraham's side. The rich man also died and was buried. In Hades, where he was in torment, he looked up and saw Abraham far away, with Lazarus by his side. So he called to him, "Father Abraham, have pity on me and send Lazarus to dip the tip of his finger in water and cool my tongue because I am in agony in this fire."
>
> But Abraham replied, "Son, remember that in your lifetime you received your good things, while Lazarus received bad things, but now he is comforted here and you are in agony. And besides all this, between us and you a great chasm has been set in place so that those who want to go from here to you cannot, nor can anyone cross over from there to us."

He answered, "Then I beg you, father, send Lazarus to my family, for I have five brothers. Let him warn them so that they will not also come to this place of torment."

Abraham replied, "They have Moses and the Prophets; let them listen to them."

"No, father Abraham," he said, "but if someone from the dead goes to them, they will repent."

He said to him, "If they do not listen to Moses and the Prophets, they will not be convinced even if someone rises from the dead." (Luke 16:19–31)

Jesus allowed us to get a glimpse of this man's eternal experience. The rich man (let's call him Richard) dressed in fine clothes and lived in a daily lap of luxury. He was probably very familiar with poor Lazarus and witnessed him picking up the scraps from the garbage. He evidently didn't put much effort into caring for his wounds, giving him shelter, or feeding him. Only the dogs would come to help.

Everything was going great for Richard until his life came to an end. The next thing we hear is that both men died. Richard's lifestyle led him straight to hell, where he was in torment. Jesus elaborates for us, "He begged, 'Father Abraham, have pity on me and send Lazarus to dip the tip of his finger in water and cool my tongue because I am in agony in this fire.'"

It is ironic that Lazarus begged Richard for food while they both lived, but now the tables have turned. In the afterlife, Richard is the one begging for Lazarus to cool his tongue from the heat of the fire. Richard wore fine linen on earth while Lazarus is now the one wearing fine linen in paradise.

Richard quickly realized he wasn't getting out and there was nothing he could do. The only thing he could do was plead for the poor man to rise from the dead and warn his brothers of the reality of hell. This request was also turned down. God was patient with Richard his entire life as he waited for him to trust in God and not his riches. Unfortunately, Richard bet on black and made the short-sighted decision.

Richard was told, "If they do not listen to Moses and the Prophets, they will not be convinced even if someone rises from the dead." In other words, we are all held accountable for what is written in God's Word. If his brothers didn't believe what was written in the Scriptures, they still wouldn't believe if Lazarus rose from the dead to warn them.

God revealed the reason for unbelief and perhaps the reason for Richards as well:

> This is the verdict: Light has come into the world, but people loved darkness instead of the light because their deeds were evil. Everyone who does evil hates the light, and will not come into the light for fear that their deeds will be exposed. (John 3:19–20)

God knew me from deep within and he knew that I had secret pleasures that held me back from giving my life to him. I subconsciously ran from him at every corner, but he compassionately pursued me because his love was so much greater than my fear. He knew that when the pain grew deep enough, perhaps I would be open to the idea that he loved and cared for me. I know beyond a shadow of a doubt that God did the same for Richard because his love is so strong and his mercies are new every morning. Unfortunately, Richard never responded and his time ran out.

Jesus's account of this story gives tremendous insight into the vivid nature of the kingdom of hell and what Richard's human experience looked and felt like. He had full memory recall, a wide array of emotions, an active conscience, and his senses were fully intact. He was able to remember his life and his loved ones as he took the time to plead for his family. He was able to sense pain, loneliness, and regret as he begged Lazarus to touch his tongue with cold water to dull the intensity of the heat. The reality of the place overwhelmed him, and he had no control over it.

Perhaps God felt that Richard's story was necessary to record, as an attempt to help some overcome the apprehensiveness of faith and cross over from death to life. The bible says in the book of Jude, that some people need to hear about God's mercy, mixed with a little fear, in order for the message to be taken to heart. For the person that responds, the end result is that they're snatched from the fire into an abundant life they've always dreamed of. What an enormous blessing in disguise. Here is how Jude puts it:

> Be merciful to those who doubt; save others by snatching them from the fire; to others show mercy, mixed with fear—hating even the clothing stained by corruptible flesh (Jude 1:22-23)

Hellish Details

There's worldwide intrigue surrounding the topic of hell. Some are fascinated with it and even go so far as to name their cities and towns after this place. Take a drive through Michigan, just south of Highway 36, and you'll find a city called Hell—complete with the "Hell Hole Bar". Take a cruise over to the Grand Cayman area of the Caribbean and you'll find another town called Hell, where you can visit the Devil's Hangout Gift Shop. If you're ever in Lanke, Norway, you can visit the village area of Hell, famous for the postcard that reads, "Before you go to Heaven, go to Hell-Norway."

These and more are all real places on the planet earth—and so is the literal kingdom of hell. According to the books of Ezekiel and Matthew, it's geographically in the "heart of the earth," somewhere within the mantle, core, or inner core of our planet. It makes total sense when you consider that hot gases and lava flow from beneath the earth's surface through the top of volcanic mountains. Scientists say the earth's core is hot because of the decay of radioactive uranium and estimate that the heart of the earth may be as hot as twelve thousand degrees.

Is It Permanent?

The book of Revelation teaches us that God will eventually create a new heaven and a new earth free of sin, as it was originally intended. Since hell is centrally located within the earth, it will be destroyed along with the old earth. All these events are described in detail in the book of Daniel and Revelation. We'll get into more of this in the last chapter when we talk about God's predictions for the end of the world as we know it in vivid detail.

After this, all of hell's occupants will be emptied out to stand before their maker without the blood of Jesus to wipe their sins away. This is the infamous day known as the *Great White Throne Judgment*, popularly known in Hollywood as "Judgment Day."

The book of Hebrews says it this way,

> People are destined to die once, and after that to face judgment. (Hebrews 9:27)

The twentieth chapter of Revelation explains it this way,

> And I saw the dead, great and small, standing before the throne, and books were opened. Another book was opened, which is the book of life. The dead were judged according to what they had done as recorded in the books. The sea gave up the dead that was in it, and death and Hades gave up the dead that was in them, and each person was judged according to what they had done. Then death and Hades were thrown into the lake of fire. The lake of fire is the second death. Anyone whose name was not found written in the book of life was thrown into the lake of fire. (Revelation 20:12–15)

If you noticed in Richard's story, he didn't have a chance to stand before God and explain anything. He had gone immediately to hell, which is like a holding cell until the endtimes are over. Richard and the rest of hell's occupants will spend some time there awaiting this trial at the great white throne judgment. Everyone—small and great, rich and poor alike—will be brought immediately before the throne of God.

What happens next? We are told that the books were opened, and the dead were judged according to what they had done. Why is that? Well, those standing before the throne of God on judgment day had rejected the work of Christ on their behalf, so they had to stand on their own righteousness. Naturally, Richard's only defense would've been "God, I was a good person" or "I did all these good things." Especially after already experiencing what hell is like, I'm sure he will try any excuse possible—I sure would.

God knew every thought that Richard had, long before he had it. He knew his motives in every situation and there was no need to explain. God simply opened the record books to reveal every thought he had behind every action.

> This will take place on the day when God judges people's secrets through Jesus Christ. (Romans 2:16)

When the record books are finally opened up, Richard will discover that nothing was hidden from God's sight and his life was being recorded. Here's what happens next:

> Then death and Hades [hell] was thrown into the lake of fire. The lake of fire is the second death. Anyone whose name was not found written in the book of life was thrown into the lake of fire. (Revelation 20:14–15)

The Lake of Fire is the second and final death. We don't know much about this place, but we do know that the judgment is final.

The greatest prize in all of human history is that our names are written in the Book of Life. This book is the list of everyone who has humbled themselves before God and had their sins washed away by the blood of Jesus. We have an amazing opportunity right now to know beyond a shadow of a doubt that our names are already written in the Book of Life. If you have not yet done this and want to, let's do it now together!

Talk to God and say something like this:

Dear Lord,

Thank you for loving me and never giving up on me. Please forgive me of all my sins past, present and future. I've been living my own way and I want to change and give my life to you. I believe you died for me and rose from the dead to save me. Thank you in advance for hearing me, loving me and forgiving me. Lord, continue to bless me and help me live your way.

In Jesus name, amen.

That's enough about hell. Let's talk about heaven.

CHAPTER 7

THE PARTY OF A LIFETIME

Verse 7

In my Father's house are many mansions: if it
were not so, I would have told you. I go to prepare a place for you. And if I go and prepare a
place for you, I will come again, and receive you
unto myself; that where I am, there ye may be
also. (John 14:2–3 KJV)

God hasn't prepared just any place for us in heaven—he has prepared
many mansions! Let's consider that for one second. How would you
feel if someone told you, "I hope you don't mind, I bought you a
special place to live. Oh, and by the way, I paid all cash, and now you
own it free and clear. The utilities and taxes are prepaid for eternity,
so just enjoy it!"

That is no fantasy; that's the reality for those who bet on red.
We will get to enjoy instant millionaire status in the next life because
of our very rich Father's love for his children. The heart of God has
always been to lavish his children with gifts. Now that sin is removed,
he finally gets to do that.

Through this chapter, we will take a closer look at what our
home will look like and uncover some of the heavenly mysteries in
store for us. Jesus said, "I go to prepare a place for you" about two

thousand years ago. Well, he's not back yet! It's reasonable to assume that he has been preparing this home of ours over the last two thousand years.

In the context of a love relationship with our Creator, this makes perfect sense. If you love something and paid a heavy price for it, wouldn't you want to give it a special home? We were an expensive purchase for God, bought with his own blood—and now he gets to finally shower us with all the amazing gifts that he has prepared.

Throughout the Bible, God labels us as his "bride." With this analogy, we see God's heart for us. As a husband myself, I love my bride and my children more than anything on earth, and I would protect them more than anyone else. God is much more loving, compassionate, and caring than I could ever be. With that incomprehensible love, God—the ultimate husband—longs to have his bride as his prized possession to come home and be with him. He just so happens to be wealthier than we can imagine, and he is extremely generous. What he has is all ours, and we are heirs in his kingdom.

> However, as it is written: "What no eye has seen, what no ear has heard, and what no human mind has conceived"—the things God has prepared for those who love him. (1 Corinthians 2:9)

Try for a second to visualize the best day of your life. Was it the day you graduated from high school or college? Was it the day you got your first car or the day your child was born? Maybe it was the day you found out you were cancer-free? Could it be the day you met the man or woman of your dreams or the day you won the lottery?

Now, what if all these things happened all in the same day? Okay, now multiply that day by a million and repeat it every single day for all eternity. If you could picture that, then you're still not even close. We are told our minds cannot even conceive how good eternity in heaven will be. What a generous and amazing God we serve.

Heaven

Heaven is mentioned hundreds of times in the Bible. God is serious about what he has planned for those who love him. Revelation, the last book in the Bible, gives us an amazing overview of heaven. Let's look at it.

All of Jesus's original disciples were killed, imprisoned, tortured, or all three. The apostle John, whom God used to write the book of Revelation, was no exception. John was one of the last living disciples of Jesus and imprisoned for his faith on the Greek island of Patmos in the late first century AD. God gave him a vision of the future, the end times, and heaven itself to share with the world.

There is a ton of action stuffed into this little twenty-two-chapter book of Revelation. Let's fast-forward to the last two chapters, 21 and 22, where we get a heavenly sneak peek. We will take it section by section, breaking it up into three distinct parts: the descent of heaven, a description of heaven, and the delight of heaven.

The Descent of Heaven

> Then I saw "a new heaven and a new earth," for the first heaven and the first earth had passed away, and there was no longer any sea. I saw the Holy City, the new Jerusalem, coming down out of heaven from God, prepared as a bride beautifully dressed for her husband. And I heard a loud voice from the throne saying, "Look! God's dwelling place is now among the people, and he will dwell with them. They will be his people, and God himself will be with them and be their God." (Revelation 21:1–3)

What a phenomenal sight this is. God gives John a vision of our new heaven and earth, starting with the description of what the capital city is going to look like. Interestingly enough, it descends, as if it's slowly unveiled like a surprise gift. God likens it to a bride in all her beauty as she walks down the aisle to meet her new husband.

I remember seeing my wife on our wedding day when she turned the corner to walk down the aisle just minutes before we exchanged our vows. Everyone in the room was speechless as they caught the first glimpse of her. Her physical beauty is enough to light up the room but add to that her beautiful smile, sparkling dress, jewelry, hair, and makeup—she was and is, absolutely captivating. Likewise, when we see our new capital city being unveiled like a bride, saying that we'll be speechless may be the understatement of the century.

John went on to say, "Look! God's dwelling place is now among the people, and he will dwell with them. They will be his people, and God himself will be with them and be their God." The God of heaven, who created us for companionship, finally gets his prize—us! After thousands of years of waiting patiently, he gets to wrap his arms around us and show all that he has prepared. Now that sin is removed, our Creator will get to hang out with us in perfect harmony.

As our new heavenly city is being lowered, John switched gears for a second to encourage those who have long awaited this heavenly experience.

> "'He will wipe every tear from their eyes. There will be no more death' or mourning or crying or pain, for the old order of things has passed away."
>
> He who was seated on the throne said, "I am making everything new!" Then he said, "Write this down, for these words are trustworthy and true."
>
> He said to me: "It is done. I am the Alpha and the Omega, the Beginning and the End. To the thirsty, I will give water without cost from the spring of the water of life. Those who are victorious will inherit all this, and I will be their

God and they will be my children. (Revelation 21:4–7)

While we may not be able to fully comprehend what heaven will be like, we are clearly told what it will not be like. There will not be any mourning, death, heartache, crying, or pain. There will be no more stress, hardship, sickness, or disease. There will be no physical or emotional pain ever again.

The human experience has been filled with all kinds of ailments, heartaches, and pain. People get cancer, babies die, kids get hurt, jobs are lost, marriages are destroyed, tragedy strikes, and terrorists attack. This "old order of things" exists because sin rules the world. Soon all the pain of this life will simply be non-existent.

Our friend John briefly paused in this heavenly discussion to go on a quick detour.

> But the cowardly, the unbelieving, the vile, the murderers, the sexually immoral, those who practice magic arts, the idolaters and all liars—they will be consigned to the fiery lake of burning sulfur. This is the second death. (Revelation 21:8)

John drops a bomb on us after all the flowery encouragement and reverted to what we covered in verse 6. Perhaps John was feeling that heaven is so real, amazing, and beautiful that he wanted to take a second for those who don't believe quite yet, to wake up and repent in order to experience this amazing sight that he's witnessing with his own eyes. We have all been, and will be, many things on this list—but the blood of Jesus has cleansed us to perfection.

The Description of Heaven

As the New Jerusalem was lowered into its resting place, John took us in for a closer look. He would now begin to unveil the outside and inside splendor of your new hometown. Try to keep in mind that he was seeing all of this in a vision thousands of years into the

future and it was probably difficult for him to describe it from a first
century AD perspective. Just imagine living in the 1900s and seeing
a vision of someone on a cell phone and a laptop computer from
the 2000s and try to describe it. That would be difficult to do—and
that's only one hundred years into the future. John was trying to
explain what he was seeing about two thousand years in the future.

> And he carried me away in the Spirit to a moun-
> tain great and high, and showed me the Holy
> City, Jerusalem, coming down out of heaven
> from God. It shone with the glory of God, and
> its brilliance was like that of a very precious jewel,
> like a jasper, clear as crystal. It had a great, high
> wall with twelve gates, and with twelve angels at
> the gates. On the gates were written the names
> of the twelve tribes of Israel. There were three
> gates on the east, three on the north, three on the
> south and three on the west. The wall of the city
> had twelve foundations, and on them were the
> names of the twelve apostles of the Lamb.
>
> The angel who talked with me had a measuring
> rod of gold to measure the city, its gates, and its
> walls. The city was laid out like a square, as long
> as it was wide. He measured the city with the rod
> and found it to be 12,000 stadia in length, and as
> wide and high as it is long. The angel measured
> the wall using human measurement, and it was
> 144 cubits thick. The wall was made of jasper,
> and the city of pure gold, as pure as glass. The
> foundations of the city walls were decorated with
> every kind of precious stone. The first foundation
> was jasper, the second sapphire, the third agate,
> the fourth emerald, the fifth onyx, the sixth ruby,
> the seventh chrysolite, the eighth beryl, the ninth
> topaz, the tenth turquoise, the eleventh jacinth,

and the twelfth amethyst. The twelve gates were
twelve pearls, each gate made of a single pearl.
The great street of the city was of gold, as pure as
transparent glass. (Revelation 21:10–21)

The Bible tells us the sun was created to light up the planet earth. Here, in God's final creation, there will be no need for the sun. God himself radiates so much light that he will illuminate the entire city with his brilliance. It is hard to imagine, but it helps me understand why sinful man can't stand in the presence of God and survive. His radiant light alone would be like trying to walk on the surface of the sun and survive—we wouldn't make it.

John began to describe a "great high wall" made of jasper stone that is clear like a diamond. The wall is 144 cubits thick. A cubit is an ancient measurement that is roughly seventeen to twenty-one inches by today's measurement standards. A rough estimate puts this wall about two hundred feet thick.

This is quite intriguing. You may have heard as I have, people, talk about their near-death experiences, describing a tunnel-like walkway with a bright light shining at the end of it. Let's assume for a moment that their experiences are real and the wall itself is two hundred feet thick. If you were walking through an opening within this thick wall and heading toward the entrance gate, you would, in fact, be walking through a tunnel. At the end of this tunnel, you would see the glory and radiance of God shining through, just as John described.

John takes us through this tunnel and describes the entrance gates to the city. These gates are constructed from a single pearl with an angel of God guarding each one. It's interesting to note that the pearl is the only precious gem made from a living creation of God, the oyster. A pearl is formed as an oyster's response to injury and irritation of a grain of sand inside the shell. In this lies a beautiful truth. The beauty of the pearl comes as a result of the oyster's suffering. Perhaps the beauty of the pearly gates of heaven comes as a result of all of our suffering in this life and of Jesus's suffering on our behalf.

The gates themselves are inscribed with the names of Israel's twelve tribes. This is also interesting because Jesus himself was a descendant from the twelve tribes of Israel and he is the very gate that we walk through to get to heaven. (John 14:6)

The foundation of the city's walls will not be poured with concrete but laid with precious stones, one on top of another. Each layer of the foundation bears the names of the twelve apostles of Jesus. These apostles were responsible for spreading the good news of God's love to the non-Jewish people around the world. The apostle's message is the very *foundational* knowledge where we get our hope of heaven.

John described the city as a perfect cube as he laid out its measurements. Twelve thousand stadia in ancient measurement equates to about 1,500 miles in length, width, and height. Just to get an idea of the actual size of this place, hop in your car and drive the 1,500-mile perimeter. Start in Minneapolis, Minnesota, and drive to the west coast all the way to Seattle, Washington. Get some sleep, grab a bite to eat then drive all the way down to San Diego, California. After another night's rest, head east to Little Rock, Arkansas, then back up to Minneapolis. That's just the perimeter of the city's ground level. You'll have to take a rocket and a spacesuit to get the top though. Currently, outer space is roughly 62 miles from the earth's surface, so you still have about 1,438 miles to go. You get the idea—this place is huge and there is plenty of room.

The entire city, including the "great street" running through the middle, will be made of pure gold. This gold is so pure that it looks like clear glass. The fact that the streets are made of gold tells me something else. All the precious metals we strive for in this life will be as plentiful in heaven as concrete is now. Don't worry if you don't have those riches now, because you'll have plenty of them later and they'll be permanent.

And further...

> I did not see a temple in the city, because the
> Lord God Almighty and the Lamb are its temple.
> The city does not need the sun or the moon to

113

shine on it, for the glory of God gives it light, and
the Lamb is its lamp. The nations will walk by its
light, and the kings of the earth will bring their
splendor into it. On no day will its gates ever be
shut, for there will be no night there. The glory
and honor of the nations will be brought into it.
Nothing impure will ever enter it, nor will anyone who does what is shameful or deceitful, but
only those whose names are written in the Lamb's
book of life. (Revelation 21:22–27)

To John and every other God-fearing person, the temple was the
single most important religious structure for all worshippers around
the ancient world. So it makes sense that he would notice there was
no temple in New Jerusalem. Sin has been removed, and God's presence is no longer in a temple because he IS the temple standing there
for us to enjoy his presence openly.

John said, "Nothing impure will ever enter it, nor will anyone
who does what is shameful or deceitful, but only those whose names
are written in the Lamb's book of life." When all of the inhabitants of
heaven repented of their sins on earth, they were deemed no longer
impure, but perfect—securing them a spot in the Lamb's book of life
and the royal celebration of a lifetime.

Revelation 21 explains a lot to us about the exterior of our capital city. Now in chapter 22, we learn more about the inside of our
new home.

Then the angel showed me the river of the water
of life, as clear as crystal, flowing from the throne
of God and of the Lamb down the middle of the
great street of the city. On each side of the river
stood the tree of life, bearing twelve crops of fruit,
yielding its fruit every month. And the leaves of
the tree are for the healing of the nations. No
longer will there be any curse. The throne of God
and of the Lamb will be in the city, and his ser-

vants will serve him. They will see his face, and his name will be on their foreheads. There will be no more night. They will not need the light of a lamp or the light of the sun, for the Lord God will give them light. And they will reign forever and ever. (Revelation 22:1–5)

In the previous chapter, John talked about the "great street" made of clear gold, and here he added to that. Down the middle of this great street runs a river of life that is also as clear as crystal. This river flows down from the throne of God through the middle of the street of gold.

On each side of the road are trees of life. If you recall, one of these trees first appeared in the Garden of Eden for Adam and Eve to live forever. Once they sinned, the way to that tree was blocked. God seems to have transplanted it here for us to enjoy the healing powers it has. Perhaps the crops from this tree will help keep us young and healthy for all eternity and to continually heal all our pain and suffering that we carried from our lives on earth.

Last, notice the last line of the previous verse: "And they will reign forever and ever."

This is not the first time in Scripture that God reveals to us that we will actually *reign* with him. We are God's children, his handiwork, his love, and his heirs. We are promised to reign as some sort of royalty living in mansions built by his own hands.

> The angel said to me, "These words are trustworthy and true. The Lord, the God who inspires the prophets, sent his angel to show his servants the things that must soon take place."
>
> "Look, I am coming soon! Blessed is the one who keeps the words of the prophecy written in this scroll."

I, John, am the one who heard and saw these things. And when I had heard and seen them, I fell down to worship at the feet of the angel who had been showing them to me. But he said to me, "Don't do that! I am a fellow servant with you and with your fellow prophets and with all who keep the words of this scroll. Worship God!"

Then he told me, "Do not seal up the words of the prophecy of this scroll, because the time is near. Let the one who does wrong continue to do wrong; let the vile person continue to be vile; let the one who does right continue to do right, and let the holy person continue to be holy." (Revelation 22:6–11)

Near the end of John's vision, he had an encounter with the angel sent to show him this heavenly vision. The angel was testifying on God's behalf that everything he was just shown is trustworthy and true—and would take place soon.

John said the one who keeps these words is blessed. *Blessed* is the word we keep seeing over and over throughout the Bible that means "happy." Happy and joyful are the people who read the book of Revelation and keep the words close to their hearts! Those who trust in these words and place their bets on red will see all these amazing things.

Delight of Heaven

Speaking of the delight of heaven, what's more delightful than a party?

Party Time Baby!

There is a reason why Jesus used the analogy of the wedding party when he described the invitation to heaven. Just imagine opening the mailbox on a Saturday afternoon and finding a 24-karat gold leaf envelope with your name on it. You carefully open it to find a diamond-bordered sheet of gold-leaf writing paper with the following message:

You're Invited

Come and enjoy the finest food and wine that money can buy
at the Royal Celebration of a Lifetime.
After the party, you will be given keys to your new mansion built
especially for you.
I've been waiting for this moment for a long time, so don't be late.
I can't wait to see you!

777 Golden Road, Kingdom of Paradise

With Love,
Your Father, the King

You are personally invited to a party fit only for royalty. This is not the kind of party where you are coming as a guest of someone else. This invitation is to celebrate Jesus's victory and your inheritance just by being a child of the King. This is no fairy tale. This is exactly what will happen to those of us who bet on red. When we become God's child, we become royalty with the King of the Universe, and he is going to throw us the most epic party the world has ever seen. Isaiah gave us a tiny glimpse into the future:

> On this mountain, the Lord Almighty will prepare a feast of rich food for all peoples, a banquet of aged wine—the best of meats and the finest of wines. (Isaiah 25:6)

Just as any amazing dad would do, God kicks off our newfound lives with a royal celebration as we feast on rich food, the best of meats, and the finest of wines.

How fine is the wine he has prepared? We have an example of that too. Jesus's first recorded miracle was at a wedding party in John 2. The wine had run out, and they asked Jesus for help. He could have said, "You guys, I am God, ya know—partying is a sin, and that is bad, bad, bad. I can't help you. GET YOUR OWN DANG WINE!" But that's not who our God is. Instead, he did this:

> Nearby stood six stone water jars, the kind used by the Jews for ceremonial washing, each holding from twenty to thirty gallons.
>
> Jesus said to the servants, "Fill the jars with water"; so they filled them to the brim.
>
> Then he told them, "Now draw some out and take it to the master of the banquet."
>
> They did so, and the master of the banquet tasted the water that had been turned into wine. He did not realize where it had come from, though the servants who had drawn the water knew. Then he called the bridegroom aside and said, "Everyone brings out the choice wine first and then the cheaper wine after the guests have had too much to drink, but you have saved the best till now."
>
> What Jesus did here in Cana of Galilee was the first of the signs through which he revealed his glory, and his disciples believed in him. (John 2:6–11)

"You have saved the best till now," said the master of the banquet to Jesus. That is precisely a picture of what Jesus has done for us—saved the finest of all food and wine for us at a royal wedding party for us in heaven. This miracle not only revealed to the disciples that Jesus was God himself, but showed his desire to give us the best of the best of all things. God's provision for us will always be better than we can do for ourselves. We are his bride, and he wants to wine and dine us if we'll let him. He's been waiting patiently ever since we were separated from him.

The world we live in is quite tricky with Satan lurking behind the scenes of humanity. He comes slithering through every means of pop culture to convince us that living a life apart from God is more fun. Satan is, in fact, a rip-off artist. While his way may satisfy our lustful pleasures for the short term, in the end, it leads to death—and all the while the real party rages in heaven.

The Homecoming Welcome

It's very difficult to comprehend the extent of God's love for us, the mercy he wants to flood upon us, and to understand that he holds no grudges against us. Oftentimes our understanding of him is not shaped from what the Bible says about him, but by the conclusions we've drawn from what we see and hear in the world around us.

Oftentimes God is mislabeled because of some Christian people in society who may not be representing him in the way we think they ought to. Perhaps God also gets a bad reputation because of all the bloody religious wars of the past or well-meaning Christian friends and family members who don't have a talent for setting the best example. Every one of us is a fallen person who sins daily, so it is impossible to judge God accurately using the barometer of human imperfection.

Instead of looking around a broken society for answers, I think it would be wise for us to learn of God's love and understand how we'll be welcomed home—the way that *he* describes it. In Luke 15, we see Jesus walking into a home full of prostitutes, cheaters, liars, and thieves—a modern-day brothel of sorts. He was ridiculed for hanging out with these people, but he loved them and went in anyway. He began to share a series of three stories called "The Lost Sheep," "The Lost Coin," and "The Lost Son" to clear up any misconceptions about how God sees us upon our return to him. Let's focus on the last one, "The Lost Son."

Jesus continued: "There was a man who had two sons. The younger one said to his father, 'Father, give me my share of the estate.' So he divided his property between them.

"Not long after that, the younger son got together all he had, set off for a distant country and there squandered his wealth in wild living. After he had spent everything, there was a severe famine in that whole country, and he began to be in need. So he went and hired himself out to a citizen of that country, who sent him to his fields to feed pigs. He longed to fill his stomach with the pods that the pigs were eating, but no one gave him anything.

"When he came to his senses, he said, 'How many of my father's hired servants have food to spare, and here I am starving to death! I will set out and go back to my father and say to him: Father, I have sinned against heaven and against you. I am no longer worthy to be called your son; make me like one of your hired servants.' So he got up and went to his father.

"But while he was still a long way off, his father saw him and was filled with compassion for him; he ran to his son, threw his arms around him and kissed him.

"The son said to him, 'Father, I have sinned against heaven and against you. I am no longer worthy to be called your son.'

"But the father said to his servants, 'Quick! Bring the best robe and put it on him. Put a ring on his finger and sandals on his feet. Bring the fattened calf and kill it. Let's have a feast and celebrate. For this son of mine was dead and is alive again; he was lost and is found.' So they began to celebrate.

"Meanwhile, the older son was in the field. When he came near the house, he heard music and dancing. So he called one of the servants and asked him what was going on. 'Your brother has come,' he replied, 'and your father has killed the fattened calf because he has him back safe and sound.'

"The older brother became angry and refused to go in. So his father went out and pleaded with him. But he answered his father, 'Look! All these years I've been slaving for you and never disobeyed your orders. Yet you never gave me even a young goat so I could celebrate with my friends. But when this son of yours who has squandered your property with prostitutes comes home, you kill the fattened calf for him!'

"'My son,' the father said, 'you are always with me, and everything I have is yours. But we had to celebrate and be glad because this brother of yours was dead and is alive again; he was lost and is found.'" (Luke 15:11–32)

Sharing this story, Jesus clearly expressed the depth of his love for you and me. The father did not ridicule or shame the son for running away, nor did he punish him. Rather, his heart was filled with joy when his son returned—and he threw a party. Jesus wanted us to know that this is precisely how God feels about us. The forgiveness he has waiting for us stretches beyond our imagination, and the celebration he's prepared for us will be mind-blowing.

Being a dad now for about twelve years, helps me to totally understand this. My wife and I have two of the best kids in the world. When they make mistakes, our love for them never dulls. Actually, sometimes the opposite occurs. At times, we can't help but simply smile on the inside when they slip up because we see ourselves in them, just learning and growing. Our love for them is unconditional and what matters most is that they are loved and come home safe and sound.

God's love for us is very similar, only much deeper. He demonstrated his amazing love for us by laying his life down so we can come home to him safe and sound. He's waiting with his arms wide open to show us all that he has prepared at the royal wedding banquet and beyond.

That about sums up the message of Betting on Red and how we win the ultimate jackpot that extends well beyond this temporary life we're living. I want to conclude our time together with one final chapter that's dedicated to the person who requires more tangible evidence that God really exists and that he actually inspired the bible above any other religious book in history. For those who want to go deeper, we're going to explore some of the physical evidence that reveal God's unique fingerprints all over the bible and the universe itself. These simple proofs will expose the divine nature of the bible and show that His simple message is mighty to rescue anyone that has a thirst for truth, peace, hope, and happiness now and forevermore.

CHAPTER 8

THE FINGERPRINTS OF GOD

The story of God's love and his constant pursuit of us is perhaps the greatest love story ever told. It is all written in the novel that outsells every other book year after year, the Bible. Perhaps this acronym says it best:

B-Basic
I-Instructions
B-Before
L-Leaving
E-Earth

Much of the content, examples, and references in this book come straight from this collection of ancient writings. Millions of people throughout the world today use the Bible as their ultimate source of information to believe in, trust in, and adhere to in order to get God's perspective on this world and the one to come. Yet, some people have wondered how the Bible compares to other religious books of faith.

If a book's content is legitimately from the creator of the universe, wouldn't there be a lot of tangible evidence to prove it? That's a big YES. God put his fingerprint, stamp, and signature all over the bible in multiple ways to prove its divine origin unlike any other religious text in circulation.

There are many scholars from the worlds of science, history, and prophecy that have gone to great lengths to uncover a countless amount of evidence that display the bible's unparalleled divine authenticity. We will briefly look at a few popular favorites—strictly from a laypersons point of view. Let's get into it.

Archaeological Evidence—The Bible's Consistency Over Time

I've always had a fascination with history since I was a little boy and only intensified since I became a believer. The more I studied, the more I found that there were solid, tangible pieces of evidence for my faith that only made my convictions that much stronger. I was excited to find that biblical events weren't only written in the pages of scripture, but spread throughout our ancient history books. An example of that was when I found that second century Roman and Greek historians like Tacitus and Thallus recorded the event of Jesus's resurrection into historical literature almost two thousand years ago.

Perhaps even more revealing than reading about past events from ancient historians, are the written historical pieces of evidence found preserved under-ground through archaeological discovery. It's pretty difficult to refute evidence that scientists have found preserved beneath the Earth's surface from centuries past. Thanks to the diligent work of the science professionals working the ground, biblical history can be confirmed with digging tools and modern technology.

Archaeology has not only revealed and confirmed history underground, but it's also helped to relieve a concern in regards to the consistency of the bible throughout time. One question that comes up from time to time was, "Has the bible changed throughout history and how accurate is it compared to the bible of the first century?" Some critics have claimed that the Bible has changed so many times through time and translation, that it's hard to know if it's the same message from thousands of years ago. Well, perhaps God miraculously addressed this concern with good old-fashioned archaeology.

One of the biggest biblical archaeological discoveries of all time was made in the winter of 1946, putting an end to the debate on the bible's consistency throughout time. Two shepherd boys of the Ta'amireh Bedouin tribe on the northwestern part of the West Bank in Qumran were chasing a stray goat near their hometown. The animal led these shepherd boys to what appeared to be ancient caves carved in limestone.

Thinking the goat had gone into one of these caves, the boys drew closer. One of the shepherds began throwing rocks in one of the caves to see how deep it was. To his surprise, he heard what sounded like pottery breaking. What Muhammed edh-Dhib didn't know was that he was about to discover a scientific goldmine of biblical proportion. Muhammed was instrumental in the discovery of eleven caves that held over 930 scrolls of historical documents. These caves looked to be the library of ancient first-century Jews.

These documents were stored in clay pots within the caves. A thorough search of the area also found ancient ruins of buildings, pottery kilns that made the pottery jars, and an ancient two-story building that contained writing benches and inkwells.

What was found on these documents? There were many manuscripts, including marriage contracts, calendars, and other personal documents pertaining to the life of this ancient Jewish tribe. These documents were written on leather parchment and papyrus in three different languages written in ancient "scroll" type format.

Further exploration of the caves found more than just ancient personal documents. What was found could be touted as the biblical discovery heard around the world. Critics of the Bible were not happy to learn that over 220 ancient biblical manuscripts were found. These manuscripts consisted of portions of every single book of the Old Testament except the book of Esther.

This discovery shocked the known world. Before this amazing find, the oldest manuscripts of the Bible dated back only to AD 1000, about one thousand years *after* Jesus walked the earth. These manuscripts were called the codices, which the versions of the Bible we have today come from. The shock came from dating these new manuscripts.

These manuscripts found in the caves were about a thousand years older than the AD 1000 manuscripts that we used to form the

Bible we use today. The newly recovered cave manuscripts were dated as far back as 300 BC and as new as AD 40, which meant they were written much closer to the biblical era than anyone ever expected.

Why is this important? Well, some scoffers of the Bible made the claim that God's original words were "lost" in translation. Their claim is that because the original text was either loosely translated, lost, or changed throughout the years, the Bible should be cast aside and left for dead. These arguments were completely put to rest with the discovery that came out of cave number one.

They found the entire book of Isaiah, which points to the coming of Jesus numerous times. The true test would be now to compare the late AD 1000 manuscripts to the ones written in the cave and see how different they were. Close examination proved that the AD 1000 scrolls were virtually identical to the ones found in the caves. The slight differences consisted of spelling alterations and slips of the pen, many no different than the words *under* and *below*. The accuracy in content was astounding, and the overall message was exactly the same.

In summary, the bible we have today was proven to be accurate through archaeological discovery. If the documents found among the caves were vastly different than the codices used to create our bible, it would be difficult to verify the accuracy of our ancient manuscripts. Perhaps God used two children and a little stray farm animal to show the world that he is faithful to keep his word pure and true over thousands of years. Despite minor slips in grammar and punctuation, the bible in our stores can be trusted for it's content and authenticity as a love letter from our Creator to his creation.

Archaeological Accuracy—Artifacts

There are literally hundreds of historical artifacts being discovered as each decade passes and many hidden treasures are added to the list every year. It's very revealing to note that the historical evidence found underground confirms and coincides with biblical history—never contradicting it. Perhaps it's even more revealing to note that many archaeological discoveries are being made by using the bible's geographical descriptions as their map to finding ancient artifacts buried underground.

There are so many more archaeological finds being discovered other than the "Dead Sea Scrolls" that were found among the caves at Qumran. Here's just one more example out of hundreds that are coming to the surface and changing the way the science world thinks about biblical history.

The Taylor Prism

In the British Museum of Bloomsbury London, you'll find about eight million objects of historical significance. One of many objects is known as the *Taylor Prism* which was discovered by Colonel Robert Taylor in 1830 in the city of Ninevah, Northern Iraq. This "prism" is a six-sided clay tablet that documents the military victories of a once proud and arrogant King Sennacherib of Assyria that has been scientifically dated back to 690 B.C. With shocking accuracy, we will clearly see these events cross-referenced in the bible perfectly with the inscriptions written on the Taylor Prism.

Taylor Prism Record-

In the documentation of his expeditions into the land of Judea, King Sennacherib inscribed this on the prism's clay surface, "I am Sennacherib the Great King, the mighty king, King of the World! As for Hezekiah the Judahite, who didn't submit to my yoke: forty-six of his strong walled cities, as well as the small towns in the area which were without number, by leveling with battering-rams and by bringing up siege engines."

Biblical Record-

2 Chronicles 32:1—"After Hezekiah had faithfully carried out this work, King Sennacherib of Assyria invaded Judah. He laid siege to the fortified towns, giving orders for his army to break through their walls."

The pompous King of Assyria also imposed heavy taxes on Judah's King Hezekiah which is also documented in the bible and cross-referenced with the Taylor Prism in perfect harmony.

The Taylor Prism Record-

"He Hezekiah, overwhelmed by my majestic awe, he sent me to Nineveh my capital, thirty talents of gold…"

Biblical Record-

2 Kings 18:14 NIV-"King Hezekiah, sent this message to the King of Assyria at Lachish: "I have done wrong. Withdraw from me and I will pay whatever you demand of me." The king of Assyria exacted from Hezekiah king of Judah three hundred talents of silver and thirty talents of gold."

We haven't begun to scratch the surface as to how biblical archeology confirms published history. If you enjoy this topic there are many resources that can be found online to research what the science world has been uncovering. A few resources that come to mind are answersingenesis.org and biblicalarchaeology.org.

Scientific Accuracy

In addition to the fascinating world of Archaeology, the bible is filled with a slew of scientific data that's just as exciting to study. Scientific data found in the bible was in print hundreds and thousands of years before scientists could validate it with modern knowledge and equipment. The more technology improves, the more the bible's scientific data is proven to be incredibly accurate.

The funny thing is that the word *science* is a Latin word for "knowledge." Science does not mean "anti-God." After all, who is more knowledgeable than God alone? God is the author and King of science, and the bible's pinpoint scientific accuracy is another layer of evidence that scripture is divinely inspired. I must say that I am very thankful to the scientists out there who believe that God is the masterful creator—not buying into the stances that the atheistic science world has. The father of modern science, Sir Isaac Newton is a perfect example.

Let's kick off our little science talk by discussing the earth itself for a second. Many years ago, scientists came to the conclusion that the earth was flat and they were adamant about it. Prior to making that assumption, perhaps they should've consulted the creator of the universe first. If they had, this is what they would've read:

> He sits enthroned above the *circle* of the earth,
> and its people are like grasshoppers. He stretches
> out the heavens like a canopy and spreads them
> out like a tent to live in. (Isaiah 40:22)

If they would've trusted in scripture, the science world would've have known the earth is round. As science and technology improve, the more they realize that the bible has many of the answers they were looking for.

Not only did the science world try to portray a flat earth, they were also convinced that there were only eleven hundred stars in the sky and that all the stars were the same size. There was also a time when science believed that the earth couldn't possibly just "float" in mid-air because of its enormous mass. They pitched the world on the idea that it was resting on the shoulders of an ancient god or a large animal. They were also sure that air itself was without weight, that winds only blew straight, that ocean waters were fed strictly by rivers and rain, the ocean floor was flat, and light itself was fixed in place. The list goes on…

Now that they've observed further and confirmed with technology, the science world believes exactly what the bible has always stated; that stars are innumerable (Jeremiah 33:22), and they are all different (1 Corinthians 15:41), the earth is free-floating in space (Job 26:7), air has weight (Job 28:25), winds blow in cyclones (Ecclesiastes 1:6), oceans have springs (Job 38:16), the ocean floor contains deep valleys and mountains (2 Samuel 22:16), and light moves (Job 38: 19-20).

If our scientific forefathers would've had a little bit more faith in the bible, they wouldn't have been surprised to find tangible signs of a creative God all over the universe. They would've known there were constellations in the sky, instead of "discovering them" (Job 38:31-32) and they wouldn't have been surprised to find dinosaur bones lying in the ground (Job 40:15-19). God has left his fingerprint all over our planet and made sure that the bible has captured many descriptions of His handiwork.

Much to the dismay of the atheistic science community, there are many scientists today who are "creationists" and would testify to the overwhelming evidence that the Earth was in-fact created just as the bible declares. For others, however, this is not "scientific enough", so they have created alternative theories to replace the biblical creation record. Enter the *big bang theory*.

The *big bang* will always remain a theory because it cannot be proven. Why? For one, there were no eyewitnesses. Second, man is fallible; incapable of knowing all things as they have already proven so with their other faulty conclusions. The science world wasn't around at the Earth's creation, so their claims require substantial evidence and there is a tremendous lack of it. As a lover of science myself, yet not a scientist, I am going to approach this big bang discussion solely from a laypersons point of view.

The big bang theory suggests that everything we see and know of today, "evolved" over *millions and millions of years* after a big explosion. When has anything been blown to shreds, only to reform and function as a complex working machine? You know…like the intricate human body and everything else that we see in nature and biology? The very function of this theory is explained away simply by saying, *millions and millions of years*, in which there is also no proof. For giggles, let's go ahead and test this theory with a little experiment and recreate the scenario to see what happens.

Let's go to the store and buy a working laptop in an attempt to recreate this explosion. I am sure we can all agree that this computer didn't just appear as a complex machine over millions of years. It was planned, designed, and built to precision in a factory. Now, let's mimic this big bang explosion and blow this thing up! What is the likelihood that over millions and millions of years, this computer will find all its own parts and put itself back together again to operate as a precision machine with no help from an intelligent designer? It would never happen, and it never happened with the universe. It will always remain a theory of man's creation.

God, in His infinite wisdom, fashioned the entire universe with all the complexities and absolute beauty and precision to show his creation that he is the Creator. The more you read about this subject, the more awesome it becomes and the more obvious it is that God is the intelligent designer who created something special for you and me. The best news of all is that the world he's building for us next will blow this current one out of the water.

Prophetic Accuracy—The Mother of All Evidence

I'd like to wrap up by sharing what many believe to be the mother of all evidence and the ultimate proof that God himself inspired the writing of the Bible—the magnificent fingerprint of prophecy.

Worldwide intrigue surrounds the idea of being able to predict the future. You may have seen talk shows where people have claimed they can tell the future or perhaps you've seen psychic shops around town and watched movies related to people with psychic abilities. Throughout history, some people have been bold in their attempts to predict the future and some have vaguely predicted a few events. The truth remains that they've been wrong a lot more than they have been right. Never in history has someone been able to make accurate predictions with one hundred percent accuracy, one hundred percent of the time.

The Bible, on the other hand, is the only exception to that rule. This ancient collection of writings has proven itself to be perfectly accurate at predicting the future. Now that much of human history has been documented for us, we can easily look back and see that prophecies that were written in the bible, were indeed fulfilled later with perfect accuracy. This achievement alone separates the Bible from all other religious texts and reveals its divine nature. After all, predicting the future perfectly can only be accomplished by the one who knows every ounce of the past, present, and future.

God gave specific men and women the gift of prophecy and roughly one-third of the entire Bible was written by these people called *prophets*. Their job was to hear the voice of God and communicate back to the people whatever he wanted them to know. They often shared words of encouragement, words of knowledge, warning, and of wisdom. These words were transcribed on scrolls of papyrus and other materials for those to read in the future and discover that God himself was the inspiration behind the words when the events came to pass.

Prophets were held to a really high standard. When God gave them a word, they had to repeat *only* what was told to them; not injecting their own interpretation or opinion. The Spirit of God was upon them while they were doing their job to keep them bold, accurate and honest. The prophet was proven to be God's mouthpiece when *every single one* of their predictions came to pass with perfect accuracy. Here are a few references to that standard:

> For prophecy never had its origin in the human will, but prophets, though human, spoke from God as they were carried along by the Holy Spirit. (2 Peter 1:21)

> If what a prophet proclaims in the name of the Lord does not take place or come true, that is a message the Lord has not spoken. That prophet has spoken presumptuously, so do not be alarmed. (Deuteronomy 18:22)

> But the prophet who prophesies peace will be recognized as one truly sent by the Lord only if his prediction comes true. (Jeremiah 28:9)

When all this comes true—and it surely will—
then they will know that a prophet has been
among them. (Ezekiel 33:33)

In the past, God spoke to our ancestors through
the prophets at many times and in various ways,
but in these last days he has spoken to us by
his Son, whom he appointed heir of all things,
and through whom also he made the universe.
(Hebrews 1:1–2)

People have tried to play copycat and predict future events, but
time always exposed the truth. When the events they predicted didn't
happen with perfect accuracy, they were exposed as illegitimate.
There have been entire religious organizations that have attempted
to predict the future yet were disproven when they weren't accurate.
They often had to backtrack, change their predictions, move the
date, and try all sorts of shenanigans when things didn't shake out as
they predicted.

Putting the Power of Prophecy in Perspective

I want to put the power of prophecy in perspective by sharing a
little fictional story and place you in it to help grasp its power.

Let's say you live in the continent of North America and the
year is AD 1500. This territory (now called the United States) was
explored by Christopher Columbus just eight years prior in 1492.
You settle in a little town outside what is known today as Boston. You
get to know your neighbors well.

One afternoon, one of your neighbors comes into your barn for
some tea by the fire. This guy loves to tell stories. One story is especially interesting. He says, "I want to tell you a true story. In 1891,
391 years from now, a man by the name of James Naismith will
invent a game called basketball. This game will be one of the most
popular pastimes in this country where we are standing, which will
be called the United States of America and will grow to fifty states by

1959. In this sport of basketball, there will be a round object called a "ball" that will be thrown into a basket originally supposed to hold peaches. The sport will grow to one of the most popular sports in the world."

Your neighbor continues his story. "There will be a team from a future state known as Minnesota. The group of players will call themselves the Lakers because this area will have over ten thousand lakes. Then in 1960, they will move from Minnesota to a state called California, and then to a specific city that they will call Los Angeles, where they will keep their name, the Lakers.

"This team will win sixteen championships and have a really good player named Kobe Bryant, who will be one of the best in history and will play his last game and retire in the year 2016."

After hearing all that, you begin to question the sanity of your neighbor, because there is really no way to verify if these things will come true or not. After he leaves, you begin to think more about his predictions and come to several possible conclusions. One is that he, without a doubt, is completely insane. Second, if there were a way to verify that these things actually did happen, this guy would be like God—knowing future events long before they happen.

You conclude there isn't a way to be transported into the future to verify his story, so you choose the next best thing. You take out a journal and copy his predictions for future relatives to verify. In 2017, your very distant relative finds the journal that had been passed through the family. It was not until centuries later that your neighbor was found to be exact in his predictions and not a lunatic at all. Everything was perfectly accurate. That's the power of prophecy.

God gave us all the hard evidence we need by writing history in advance. He knew that when we looked at the history books and found that events were perfectly predicted, it would be revealed that he is the direct inspiration behind the Bible and worthy of our trust without a shadow of a doubt.

Now that's just a little fictional idea of the power that prophecy brings to the table. There are so many cool prophecies laced throughout scripture that are nothing short of miraculous. Let's go through a few of them and conclude our time together by scanning through a few prophecies in the "end times" that will reveal how the last days of human history will play out in marvelous detail.

Prophecy Fulfilled in History

The prophetic book of Malachi was the last book written and completed the Old Testament in the 400-500 B.C. Historical record shows us that the Old Testament, complete with all prophecies within them, was translated into the Greek language called the "Septuagint" in the third century B.C. This tells us that every prediction within the Old-Testament was in print for all to see several centuries before Jesus stepped foot onto the Earth in the first century AD.

For the Biblical prophets to put their predictions in writing for all to scrutinize for the next hundreds and thousands of years, either made them a little coo-coo or completely confident that they heard from God himself. History has proven the latter. We now can look back and see that every single prophecy of history has come to fruition.

The world kept a strict eye on many prophecies, but one group of predictions stands out above the rest—the passages that foretold the coming of God himself as the Savior and King to the world stage. Over three hundred Old Testament prophecies pointed to the birth of a baby boy who would be King and called "Wonderful Counselor, Mighty God, the Everlasting Father, the Prince of Peace" (Isaiah 9:6).

Little did the watching world know, the first-century believers were living in the very generation that would see these predictions come to fruition before their very eyes. Here are just a few of the written prophecies that people living in the first century would have been reading while they awaited the arrival of their Savior.

The Saviors Divine Origin and Specific Birthplace

The divine origin of the Savior was perhaps one of the most intriguing of them all. The concept of the creator God coming down in human flesh was uncharted territory, awe-inspiring, and miraculous to say the least. These predictions came from the pen of the prophets Micah and Isaiah about seven hundred years before Christ walked the earth. Let's look at a few of them.

> "Therefore the Lord himself will give you a sign: The virgin will conceive and give birth to a son, and will call him Immanuel (which means 'God with us'). (Isaiah 7:14 NLT) Written about 735 BC

> "For to us a child is born, to us, a son is given, and the government will be on his shoulders. And he will be called Wonderful Counselor, Mighty God, Everlasting Father, Prince of Peace. Of the greatness of his government and peace, there will be no end." (Isaiah 9:6-7) Written about 735 BC

> "But you, Bethlehem Ephrathah, though you are small among the clans of Judah, out of you will come for me one who will be ruler over Israel, whose origins are from of old, from ancient times."(Micah 5:2) Written about the 8th century B.C.

The Savior was to be "God with us" in human flesh, born through the womb of a virgin woman showing that he was of divine origin—not born from the seed of a man. Micah's prophecy predicts he'll be from a very specific family line of the Jewish heritage—Judah. His origins are predicted to be from old and "ancient times"—that is, before the foundations of the earth to be exact. Jesus referred to himself as God, allowed others to call him God, and openly accepted worship as God. As we'll see, Jesus was born from Judah, in the town of Bethlehem in perfect harmony with prophecy.

In fulfillment of this prophecy, we'll see that when Jesus was still a baby, word traveled that the star from the east had come, signaling his arrival. There is no doubt that this disturbed the jealous ruler over that region, King Herod. Herod consulted Old Testament prophecy to find where the newborn King was to be born in an attempt to kill him so he wouldn't be a future threat to his throne. Let's take a look at these predictions from the book of Matthew:

> (Matthew 2:1-12) After Jesus was born in Bethlehem in Judea, during the time of King Herod, Magi from the east came to Jerusalem and asked, "Where is the one who has been born king of the Jews? We saw his star when it rose and have come to worship him." When King Herod heard this he was disturbed, and all Jerusalem with him. When he had called together all the people's chief priests and teachers of the law, he asked them where the Messiah was to be born. "In Bethlehem in Judea," they replied, "for this is what the prophet has written: 'But you, Bethlehem, in the land of Judah, are by no means least among the rulers of Judah; out of you will come for me one who will be ruler over Israel.'" Then Herod called the Magi secretly and found out from them the exact time the star had appeared. He sent them to Bethlehem and said, "Go and search carefully for the child. As soon as you find him, report to me, so that I too may go and worship him."(murder him would've been more honest) After they had heard the king, they went on their way, and the star they had seen when it rose went ahead of them until it stopped over the place where the child was. When they saw the star, they were overjoyed. On coming to the house, they saw the child with his mother Mary, and they bowed down and worshipped him. They opened their treasures and presented him with gifts of gold, frankincense, and myrrh. And being warned in a dream not to go back to Herod, they returned to their country by another route."

Performer of Miracles-

The Savior was predicted to reveal his divine nature by doing what no man has ever been able to do in history—perform miraculous signs as foretold by Isaiah the prophet about the 8th century B.C.

> "Say to those with fearful hearts, 'Be strong, and do not fear, for your God is coming to destroy your enemies. He is coming to save you.' And when he comes, he will open the eyes of the blind and unplug the ears of the deaf. The lame will leap like a deer and those who cannot speak will sing for joy. Springs will gush forth in the wilderness and streams will water the wasteland." (Isaiah 35: 4-6 NLT)

Jesus fulfilled this precisely. Even now, two thousand years later, Jesus is known throughout the world as the "miracle worker". His miracles weren't confined to healing ailments of the human body; they went much further. Eyewitnesses documented him calming storms, walking on the water, raising the dead, feeding thousands by multiplying a child's lunch basket, turning water into wine, restoring a man's ear that had been cut off by one of his own overzealous disciples, causing demons to beg and tremble—the list goes on. Jesus has separated himself from anyone in human history by his majestic power to control the forces of nature for the benefit of his creation that he loves.

The King would reveal himself to the world by riding in on a donkey.

> "Rejoice greatly, Daughter Zion! Shout Daughter Jerusalem! See, your king comes to you, righteous and victorious, lowly and riding on a donkey, and on a colt, the foal of a donkey.'" (Zechariah 9:9) Written about 520 BC.

As Jesus and his disciples walked along the road nearing Jerusalem, he sent a few of his disciples ahead of him to the next village. Jesus said that they would find a donkey and her colt tied together in the village ahead. He told them, "Untie them and bring them to me. If anyone says anything to you, say that the Lord needs them, and he will send them right away." This took place to fulfill what was spoken through the prophet: "Say to Daughter Zion, 'See your king comes to you, gentle and riding on a donkey, and on a colt, the foal of a donkey.'" (Matthew 21: 2-5)

This prophecy was fulfilled with precise accuracy and Zechariah goes one step further in the very next verse by revealing the King's mission:

> "I will take away the chariots from Ephraim and the warhorses from Jerusalem, and the battle bow will be broken. He will proclaim peace to the nations. His rule will extend from sea to sea and from the River to the ends of the earth."
> (Zechariah 9:10)

The Jewish people in the third decade AD lived under the rule and oppression of the Roman Empire and they were fed up. They desperately wanted their long-awaited King to liberate them from the vicious control of the Roman government and restore peace to the land. Perhaps they thought their liberation would come from their King's use of military power. They missed the point. Zechariah says here that the King wouldn't come with objects of war, but would come proclaiming a way of peace for all nations.

It seems that God had his priorities set perfectly. While the oppression of the Jewish people was important to him, he wanted to tackle the biggest oppressor of all—our sin. God's priority was to send a true King to the world stage who would give us eternal peace by single-handedly destroying the effect of sin by taking the consequences upon himself.

When it became obvious to the spectators that Jesus was not going to save them from the Roman Empire's oppression, they turned on him, mocked him, spit on him, and eventually crucified him. Little did they know they were single-handedly fulfilling our next set of prophecies—sentencing him to certain death.

I must say here that our God is forever gracious, kind, and merciful to those who don't yet believe, including the Jewish nation. Although many Jewish people have yet to recognize Jesus as their Savior, many have, like those in the *Jews for Jesus* organization. God has made a scriptural promise that he will continue to reveal himself and protect them from the destruction to come in the "end-times" that we will get into here in a few minutes.

The Savior's Prophetic Final Moments— Betrayal, Rejection, Torture, and Murder

Judas Iscariot was one of the infamous "twelve" closest friends and disciples of Jesus. The bible tells us that Judas started the time clock toward Jesus's death by giving up his night-time location to the jealous religious leaders in order for them to make a secret arrest. The chief priests agreed with this betrayal by giving Judas exactly thirty pieces of silver in exchange for the information. (Matthew 26:14-16)

Jesus knows that his days are numbered and calls for a final dinner with his closest friends. At this infamous, *Last Supper*, Jesus tells the whole group that he will be betrayed by one of his friends sitting at the table; specifically, the one that was about to share the bread bowl with him. Judas recognized that he was the one and said, "Surely you don't mean me..." and Jesus confirmed that it was him. Satan entered Judas at that moment and the two began to carry out their plan in selling out the Son of God that would ultimately lead to death. (Matthew 26: 20-25)

The story goes on that Judas would feel so bad for his betrayal, that he tried to give the money back by throwing it into God's house (the temple) and returning it back to the chief priests who made the deal. The priests thought it would be too much of sin to take back blood money, but ok to have Jesus killed. In fulfillment of prophecy, they ended up using the money to buy a pottery field; to be used as cemetery land to bury foreigners. (Matthew 27: 3-10)

All of these events were predicted centuries earlier by Zechariah and the Psalmist:

> "Even my close friend, someone I trusted, one who shared my bread, has turned against me." (Psalm 41:9)

And…

> I told them, "If you think it best, give me my pay; but if not, keep it." So they paid me thirty pieces of silver. And the Lord said to me, "throw it to the potter"—the handsome price at which they valued me! So I took the thirty pieces of silver and threw them to the potter at the house of the Lord. (Zechariah 11:12-13) Written in the sixth century BC.

Now we move onto the prophetic passages that predict the arraignment, torture, and murder of the Savior. There are so many predictions in this category, I think it would be best for anyone that is interested to look up the entire chapters of Isaiah 53 and Psalm 22. I was amazed to read the bone-chilling play by play of Jesus' arraignment, torture, and crucifixion in these two chapters alone—written hundreds of years before he was born.

These prophecies are so shockingly accurate, that some critics have even claimed that the disciples must have written the bible after Jesus's death to make sure everything lines up. This argument has been beaten back with an enormous amount of evidence. The most basic of which is that the entire Old Testament has already been proven to be in print hundreds of years before the disciples were born. Secondly, death by crucifixion as described in Psalm 22: 14-18, wasn't even invented at the time it was written. Here is a small section of that prophecy:

"I am poured out like water, and all my bones are out of joint. My heart has turned to wax; it has melted within me. My mouth is dried up like a potsherd, and my tongue sticks to the roof of my mouth; you lay me in the dust of death. Dogs surround me, a pack of villains encircles me; they pierce my hands and my feet. All my bones are on display; people stare and gloat over me." (Psalm 22: 14-18) Written about 700-1000 BC.

The picture of the crucifixion is painted clearly for us as we see a dehydrated Jesus, hanging as a display for all to see. Villians were surrounding him, "gloating", or staring upon his misfortune with a sense of pride in their achievements. His arms and legs—no doubt—pulled out of joint as far as they would go, in order to hammer in the large metal spikes through his hands and feet to keep him in position.

As you read through Psalm 22 and Isaiah 53, you'll see many more details of Jesus's dreaded final moments. The prophets predicted his silence during the trial before death, his famous words from the cross, "My God, My God, why have you forsaken me", down to the detail of the crowd "casting lots" or rolling the dice to see who would get his clothing that was pulled from him.

Isaiah goes on to give us the reason for his torture, "Surely he took up our pain and bore our suffering, yet we considered him punished by God, stricken by him, and afflicted. But he was pierced for our transgressions, he was crushed for our iniquities; the punishment that brought us peace was on him, and by his wounds, we are healed". (Isaiah 53:4-5) God's fingerprint of prophecy made the Savior's death and mission crystal clear.

There are more than three hundred prophecies of the coming Savior. These very specific predictions foretold where he would live, what type of things he would do, what agony he would endure, how he would die, and ultimately what would be accomplished at his death and resurrection. The likelihood of a person fulfilling just eight out of three hundred of them is extremely difficult, if not impossible. How difficult? The odds are said to be about 1:10 to the seventeenth power. To understand those odds, put a red "x" on a specific silver dollar and then bury it within the entire state of Texas, stacked two feet high full of silver dollars. Next, parachute out of a moving plane flying over Texas to find that specific coin on the first try—blindfolded. This may sound near impossible to find, and that's only eight fulfilled predictions. Jesus fulfilled all three hundred of them perfectly.

The Ticking Clock—Prophecy of the Last Days

Who doesn't like a good apocalyptic "Armageddon" type flick on T.V.? Some of the best movies ever made have to do with some sort of "end of days" drama. I've seen them range from a huge tidal wave crashing into New York City, to a rampant incurable virus threatening the globe, to a nuclear bomb that starts to spread fatal gases through the earth's atmosphere.

Interestingly enough, the bible has no shortage of predictions about the end of days and the apocalyptic events that follow. Given the track record of historical prophecy, I would venture to guess that future prophecy will be fulfilled just as its historic predecessor did with pinpoint accuracy.

The John and Daniel Tag Team

The story of earths' last days comes largely from the book of Daniel the prophet written in the sixth century BC and the book of Revelation written by John in the late first century AD—with some of their predictions re-iterated by Jesus himself. Daniel and John lived about seven hundred years apart from each other, yet their predictions correlate perfectly and collectively predict the end of Earth as we know it. Due to the amount of detail and imagery contained in Daniel and Revelation, end times events can be studied for years and highly recommend doing so as there is a lot that we can't cover in this short section. For the sake of brevity and clarity, we'll scratch the surface and highlight some of the main points and try to keep them in chronological order.

First, the Bible makes a very strong case that there will be a "rapture", or taking away of those who have put their faith in Jesus prior to any judgment on earth in the last days. God never appoints his children to wrathful judgment. God has exemplified this when he spared Noah and family in the moments before the world-wide flood judgment in Genesis 7 and how he saved Lot and his family before a city-wide judgment upon Sodom and Gomorrah in Genesis 19. Jesus himself explains this rapture in Matthew 24:36-44:

> "As it was in the days of Noah, so it will be at the coming of the Son of Man. For in the days before the flood, people were eating and drinking, marrying and giving in marriage, up to the day Noah entered the ark; and they knew nothing about what would happen until the flood came and took them all away. That is how it will be at the coming of the Son of Man. Two men will be in the field; one will be taken and the other left. Two women will be grinding with a hand mill; one will be taken and the other left. Therefore keep watch, because you do not know on what day your Lord will come."

I hold the belief of many others, that the departing of the saints will kick off the time known as the "last days". This is the final seven years of Earth as we now know it with Israel as the geographical focal point. This seven-year period will begin when an extremely charismatic political leader emerges on the world scene and makes a "covenant with many" for seven years; a sort of a world peace treaty.

The first half of the seven years will be amazing. This political ruler will somehow find a way to bring peace to the world—even to the war in the middle-east. The Jewish-Muslim conflict will seem to be resolved when the third Jewish temple (the holy place) will finally be re-built after almost two thousand years of lying desolate. Jewish temple sacrifices will be restored and the Jews will think this political ruler is their long-awaited savior. The Temple Institute in Israel has already prepared the artifacts of worship and are ready to move them into their new temple as soon as it's rebuilt.

Prophecy tells us that this political ruler will break the peace treaty at the midpoint of the seven years. This event starts the time clock for the destructive last half of the seven-year period, also called the "great tribulation" period. This ruler will enter the temple and defile it somehow. He'll demand to be worshipped as God himself. (Daniel 9:27)(Matthew 24:15-22)

This political ruler is known as the "beast of the sea", and will come out of many "peoples, multitudes, nations, and languages". (Revelation 17:15) This political beast is powered by Satan himself to deceive the entire world—but he is not alone. To replicate his version of the Father, Son, and Holy Spirit, Satan (the dragon) invokes his very own religious prophet known as the "beast of the earth". This religious beast and so-called "prophet" will use his spiritual swagger to mandate that the entire world worship the political beast as their savior. This is all detailed out in Revelation 13 and clarified further in Revelation 17.

Revelation goes on to say that the beast has ten horns with crowns on them and these are "ten kings that will receive a kingdom with authority (Revelation 17:12) among seven heads or 'empires'". This confederation of kings exist for one sole purpose—to give their power and authority to the beast (Revelation 17:13). It's fairly easy to speculate that a confederation of ten Kings that comes out of many nations could easily be the United Nations with the beast their leader. On the same speculative note, a great candidate for the religious leader that causes all to worship this man could very well be a wayward pope. Many people revere the office of pope and he's somewhat of a religious figurehead throughout the European world.

This demonic duo of the prophet and world leader are about to gain even more popularity. The false religious prophet was given demonic power to perform miraculous signs in order to get the world to worship the beast and deceive all the inhabitants of the earth. How miraculous will his power be? He'll be able to call fire down from heaven and he's given awesome powers to heal. The beast himself will suffer a fatal head wound. The false prophet will use his power to raise the beast from the dead to mimic the resurrection of Christ in plain view for the entire world to see. Without the recent technology of television, this wouldn't have been possible. The world will be filled with awe and wonder and they will worship the beast during these last three and a half years.

These guys will thrive on their short-lived power and cause all people, small and great, rich and poor, free and slave, to receive a mark on their right hands or on their foreheads. They will not be able to buy or sell anything unless they have the mark; more infamously known as the *mark of the beast*. Anyone that refuses to take the mark or worship this man will be hunted and killed. Here is how John describes it:

> "Then I saw a second beast, coming out of the earth. It had two horns like a lamb, but it spoke like a dragon. It exercised all the authority of the first beast on its behalf and made the earth and its inhabitants to worship the beast, whose fatal wound had been healed. And it performed great signs, even causing fire to come down from heaven to the earth in full view of the people. Because of the signs, it was given the power to perform on behalf of the first beast, it deceived the inhabitants of the earth. It ordered them to set up an image in honor of the beast who was wounded by the sword and yet lived. The second beast was given the power to give breath to the image of the first beast so that the image could speak and cause all who refused to worship the image to be killed. It also forced all people, great and small, rich and poor, free and slave, to receive a mark on their right hands or on their foreheads, so they cannot buy or sell unless they had the mark, which is the name of the beast or the number of its name. This calls for wisdom. Let the person who has insight calculate the number of

the beast, for it is the number of man. That number is 666. (Revelation 13:1-18)

John explains this as a "mark" as he is seeing this vision in the
first century. Fast forward just under two thousand years and we're
living in a technological world where microchip implants in the
human skin have become a grave reality. Imagine not being able to
buy any food, water, or clothing unless you had this mark within
your skin knowing you'll be beheaded if you refused. This sort of
technology would have sounded crazy a hundred years ago but it's
right in front of us.

At this point, the saints are long gone, the beast and his false
prophet have risen to power, world devastation is happening simultaneously (we'll cover this next) and Satan thinks he has won. Well,
he's wrong. God is always in the business of saving lives. While this is
all going on, God launches his own three-part offensive plan to warn
and save everyone that will listen.

God's first counter strike is the deployment of two, supernaturally protected individuals that will be given power to preach the
good news to the world and they're given power to destroy anyone
that comes near to harm them for three and a half years. Second,
God deploys one hundred forty four thousand "super-powered"
preachers to do the same thing, but this group is mobile and can get
to God-inspired strategic locations. Finally, God provides a supernatural witness in the form of a mighty angel that moves through the
air and proclaims the good news of Jesus—urging people not to take
the mark of the beast in order to be saved. (Revelation 7) (Revelation
11:1-11) (Revelation 13:1-14) The efforts of God's three-fold plan
resulted in saving the souls of so many people among all the blood-
shed that they were literally uncountable. (Revelation 7:9-10).

The beast goes on his own offensive. Knowing his days are really
short, his army attacks the remnant of Israel in retaliation against
God himself. They are supernaturally protected in a secure desert
location amongst caves and nourished for the entirety of the three
and a half year period. (Revelation 12:6) It's interesting to research
the desert city of Petra in Jordan. This area is in the mountain region,

just outside of Israel that may be the perfect location to hide millions of people among the seemingly endless cave structures.

Seven Seals, Seven Trumpets, and Seven Bowl Judgments on the Earth

Chronologically, we're still at the midpoint of the great tribulation period and we'll progress pretty quickly at this point. The beast is now on the throne causing political chaos on the land for the next three and half years, but now the time has come that many have feared for centuries—catastrophic destruction from above. Over two billion people will die by seven seal judgments, seven trumpet judgments, and seven bowl judgments upon the earth.

Although the sequence of these judgments has been debated, we're promised that they will happen nonetheless. I share the opinion of many, that the first seal, first trumpet, and first bowl judgment, are all the same event; followed by the second, third, fourth, and so on—just explained from a different point of view. The seal judgments appear to be the point of view as it appears in heaven, the trumpet judgments appear to be the point of view as it appears on the earth, and the bowl judgments appear to be the description of how the judgment physically affected the human population. Let's see how it breaks down this way.

The first seal (Revelation 6:1-2), first trumpet (Revelation 8:7) and first bowl judgment (Revelation 16:1-2), collectively paint a picture that begins with the imagery of the beast on a white horse with a crown and a bow—no arrow, sent out to conquer. This ruler doesn't take an offensive role at first (no bow), but rules to conquer nonetheless. At that moment, a third of the earth is burned up with what looks like hail and fire falling from the sky. A "nasty and terrible sore appeared" on those who have taken the mark of the beast.

The second seal (Revelation 6:3-4), trumpet (Revelation 8:8-9) and bowl judgment (Revelation 16:3) continue as John sees a fiery red horse with a corresponding "huge mountain burning with fire" being thrown into the sea. The massive size of this thing kills a third of the sea creatures and every other living organism; giving the waters a blood-like appearance. This asteroid-like object was so expansive, that one-third of all the ships were destroyed on the spot. Peace is taken from the earth and men begin to turn on each other with the "sword" in murderous fashion.

The third seal (Revelation 6:5-6), trumpet (Revelation 8:10-11) and bowl judgment (Revelation 16:4-7) advance with the vision of a black horse. The rider of the horse held a pair of scales in his hand that represented a severe famine that was about to sweep across the earth. A "great star" fell like a torch from heaven falling on a third of all the freshwater rivers and springs so that the water became bitter with a blood-like appearance. The former set of judgments affected the saltwater and now the freshwater supply is affected. A severe famine strikes as the lack of freshwater limits farmland crop growth and the supply of world-wide drinking water.

The fourth seal (Revelation 6:7-8), trumpet (Revelation 8:12-13) and bowl judgment (Revelation 16:8-9) follow as John sees the vision of a pale green horse. The rider of the horse was named Death, and Hades was following close behind. They were given power over a fourth of the earth to kill by sword, famine, and plague that has developed. It's added here that the "wild animals of the earth" also begin to kill mankind. Perhaps due to the lack of food and water, the land animals begin to turn and feed on their human counterparts. A third of the sun, moon, and stars were struck so a third of the earth lost its light—also affecting crops. The sun was struck in such a way that the light was lost in one area, yet intensified in another— burning people with fire. After all of this, people "cursed God" and refused to submit to his rescue plan.

There are no more horses, but John turns his eyes to heaven as the fifth seal (Revelation 6:9-11) is revealed. He quickly notices all of those who have died for the cause of faith and have not taken the mark of the beast during this great tribulation period. John says, "I saw under the alter those who had been slaughtered on account of the word of God and the witness they have given. They cried out with a loud voice, 'Holy and true Master, how long will you wait before you pass judgment? How long before you require justice for our blood, which was shed by those who live on the earth?'" Each of

SHAWN WARD

them was given a white robe, and they were told to rest just a little bit longer until the rest of them have come into the kingdom of God.

The fifth trumpet (Revelation 9:1-12) and bowl judgment (Revelation 16: 10-11) is poured out. A huge crack in the earth opened up exposing what appears to be hell itself from the heart of the earth and gushes such an enormous amount of smoke that the sun and the air were filled with darkness once again. Some sort of demonic forces were allowed to hurt the inhabitants of the earth with pain and sores, but not kill them. They suffered for five months. Again, they cursed God and still did not repent. These forces were not allowed to touch the 144,000 super-powered preachers that were still bringing in the remaining people into the kingdom of God.

The sixth seal (Revelation 6:12-17), trumpet (Revelation 9:13-21) and bowl judgment (Revelation 16:12-14) was poured out and leads us to the setting up of the infamous "Battle of Armageddon" that takes place in the desert valley of Megiddo outside of Jerusalem. Many think that this battle is synonymous with all the aforementioned judgments, however, it's quite different. This battle that we'll see take place is when justice is served—the beast and false prophet are ultimately defeated and thrown alive into the lake of fire. The deadly three and half year period is now nearing the end.

At the opening of the sixth seal judgments the "big one" hits— an earthquake so large that every mountain and island was moved from its place. The moon turns red as blood, the sun loses its light completely, stars fall from the heavens as the sky itself is "rolled up like a scroll." People hid from the wrath from above as they cried, "Fall on us and hide us from the face of the one seated on the throne and from the Lambs wrath! The great day of their wrath has come, and who is able to stand?" The great day of the Lord has finally come, where Jesus himself will go into battle and destroy the opposition.

During the preparation of the sixth judgments and the start of this great battle of Armageddon, John sees the evil spirits come from the dragon, beast and the false prophet. These evil spirits were the forces that empowered them to perform all of the miraculous signs that deceived many nations. These spirits were released unto the "kings of the east" to instigate them to form an army of two hundred million soldiers to wage war against God himself and his people. The "big one" shook the earth in such a way that it caused the great river Euphrates to dry up so this army can march through to Jerusalem on dry land. This massive army is headed for the battle of their lives that they're sure to lose.

John sees this great battle in a vision just about two thousand years ago. Not really knowing how to describe the weapons of modern warfare, he uses a lot of imagery that sounds eerily like modern battle tanks and heavy artillery. John describes, "The number of the cavalry troops was two hundred million. I heard their number. And this is the way I saw the horses and their riders in the vision: they had breastplates that were fiery red, dark blue, and as red as sulfur. The horses' heads were like lions' heads, and out of their mouths came fire, smoke, and sulfur. By these plagues a third of humankind was killed: by fire, smoke and sulfur coming out of their mouths..." As this army of two hundred million soldiers continue on their destructive path, they pass through the valley of Megiddo and meet an opponent they wished they'd never met; it's time for them to meet their maker.

John picks up in Revelation 19:11-21:

> "I saw heaven standing open and there before me was a white horse, whose rider is called Faithful and True. With justice, he judges and wages war. His eyes are like blazing fire, and on his head are many crowns. He has a name written on him that no one knows but he himself. He is dressed in a robe dipped in blood, and his name is the Word of God. The armies of heaven were right along with him, riding on white horses and dressed in fine linen, white and clean. Coming out of his mouth is a sharp sword with which to strike down the nations. He will rule them with an iron scepter. He treads the winepress of the fury of the wrath of God Almighty. On his robe and on his thigh he has this name written: King of Kings

and Lord of Lords. And I saw an angel standing in the sun, who cried in a loud voice to all the birds flying in mid-air, 'Come, gather together for the great supper of God, so that you eat the flesh of kings, generals, and the mighty, of horses and their riders, and the flesh of all people, free and slave, great and small." Then I saw the beast and the kings of the earth and their armies gathered together to wage war against the rider on the horse and his army. But the beast was captured and with it the false prophet who had performed the signs on its behalf. With these signs he had deluded who had received the mark of the beast and worshipped its image. The two of them were thrown alive into the fiery lake of burning sulfur. The rest were killed with the sword coming out of the rider on the horse, and all the birds gorged themselves on their flesh."

This scene seems as though it could come straight from an episode of Game of Thrones. The one true King, Jesus Christ himself, will come through and slaughter his enemies in one shot. The birds of the air will feast on the flesh of the evil forces that have risen against the King and his people. Revelation 14:20 says that the blood spilled in this battle will rise up to the "horses bridle", which is about four to five feet high over the 180-mile section of this Valley of Megiddo.

The seventh seal (Revelation 8:1-5), trumpet (Revelation 11:15-19) and bowl (Revelation 16:17-21) are introduced and there is silence in heaven for thirty minutes. All the prayers from all his children rose up before God like incense and their prayers are answered— the time of suffering is nearing its end. One more judgment will follow in a final attempt to get people to repent and be saved for eternity. There were "voices, lightning, thunder" and hailstones fell from heaven along with the largest earthquake—bigger than the last. This one completely removes the existence of the islands and mountains. Despite God's chastening, many refused to turn to Him—but cursed him because of the hundred-pound hailstones that pummeled the earth. The long-awaited battle of Armageddon and three and half year tribulation period are over.

We immediately progress into chapter twenty of the book of Revelation. This chapter takes us behind the scenes to the period of time immediately following the battle of Armageddon and before our grand and glorious entrance into the new heaven and new earth that John talked about earlier.

This really unique time is known as the "millennium". This is a thousand-year period that begins with Satan being bound in chains—not to deceive, control, or influence people in any way. Jesus himself, takes control of the earth and rules and reigns with those who refused to take the mark of the beast and died for their faith during the great tribulation. (Revelation 20:1-6)

The prophet Isaiah gives us a little glimpse into this time period;

> "The wolf will live with the lamb, the leopard will lie down with the goat, the calf and the lion will eat together; and a little child will lead them. The cow will feed with the bear, their young will lie down together, and the lion will eat straw like the ox. The infant will play near the cobra's den, and the young child will put its hand into the vipers' nest. They will neither harm nor destroy on my holy mountain, for the earth will be filled with the knowledge of the LORD as the waters cover the sea. In that day the root of Jesse (Jesus) will stand as a banner for the peoples; the nations will rally to him, and his resting place will be glorious. In that day the Lord will reach out his hand a second time to reclaim the surviving remnant of his people..."(Isaiah 11:1-11)

There will be many people that survive the great tribulation period, they will have kids and their children's children will have children. These generations of people will get to experience what ultimate peace on earth really looks like with Jesus himself reigning on the throne. Belief in God will no longer be a debatable topic—for they will see him face to face. While we are not sure the exact reason for this time period, we know that God is giving mankind the opportunity to see what life is like with God himself in their midst once again. Although these generations will see him face to face, they still must choose follow him. The millennial period is very similar to that of the first garden paradise; only without Satan as a factor.

Some have said, "If Satan was never around to tempt Adam and Eve in the garden, they would've never rebelled." Well soon see, this millennial period will prove that's not true. After the thousand years are up, Satan is released back to the garden of the earth for the final time. He'll gather one final army of those who hate God and array them in battle. After being in prison for a thousand years, this is his final effort to overthrow his creator from the throne and get the power that he's been craving. This foolish army and their expression of freewill will expose the rebellion that brewed in their hearts while Satan wasn't around.

Satan is released and gathers his army from the "four corners of the earth"; an army so big that "the number is as the sand of the sea". This army comes from all over the earth and surrounds the city of Jerusalem and the entire camp of God's people in the area. There is no fight. Fire rains down from heaven and devours the army instantaneously. It's all over and the King has prevailed once and for all. (Revelation 20:7-9)

Evil men are rid from the earth, and now it's Satans turn:

> "And the devil that deceived them was thrown in the lake of burning sulfur, where the beast and the false prophet had been thrown. They were tormented day and night forever and ever. Then I saw a great white throne and him who was seated on it. The earth and heavens fled from his presence, and there was no place for them. And I saw the dead, the great and small, standing before the throne, and books were opened. Another book

was opened, which is the book of life. The dead were judged according to what they had done as recorded in the books. The sea gave up the dead that was in it, and death and Hades gave up the dead that was in them, and each person was judged according to what they had done. Then death and Hades were thrown into the lake of fire. The lake of fire is the second death. Anyone whose name was not found written in the book of life was thrown into the lake of fire."(Revelation 20:10-15)

End times prophecy comes full circle to our discussion earlier of John's vision of the final Great White Throne Judgment. The names of all of those who have placed their trust in the blood of Jesus Christ alone were found in the book of life and get to experience the eternal paradise promised to them. Immediately after the judgments are poured out—everyone, everything, including hell itself was thrown into the lake of fire as chapter twenty one opens with the magnificent picture of our new home. The rest is history.

Wrapping It Up

When will the rapture take place and these things begin? We don't know for sure, but we do have a few clues. First, Israel had to be re-gathered to their homeland. The Roman Empire destroyed the temple in Jerusalem in 70 AD and dispersed the entire nation for almost two thousand years. Multiple prophecies foretold that they would return—and they would have to, in order for the Anti-Christ to negotiate a peace treaty with them and orchestrate the rebuilding of their temple.

The world was shocked to see this prophecy fulfilled on May 14th, 1948 as Israel's first Prime Minister, David Ben-Gurion declared the establishment of the Jewish State once again. Israel was immediately attacked by the armies of Iraq, Egypt, Syria, Lebanon, and Jordan, but they miraculously prevailed. They have been the only nation in history to be re-gathered after centuries of being dispersed. The likelihood of this happening would be similar to the American Indians being re-gathered to reclaim the United States for themselves after centuries of being dispersed.

One of the final clues that helps to signal the closeness of the end times comes from Daniel the prophet when he said near the end-times, "many will go here and there to increase knowledge." (Daniel 12:4) I could be wrong, but this sounds like the rampant increase in technology. Technology used to take decades to improve, but now it takes months, weeks, and even days. We're getting to the point that tech is oftentimes outdated before it's even released. For the first time in human history, we are seeing the astronomical rise of biological technology to the extent that microchips are being implanted under the human skin in Sweden for the sake of convenience. We will have to see how this technology progresses.

Whether or not we're days, weeks, months, or years away from the end is sort of irrelevant. If we all place our bets on red now, we have absolute assurance that our names are written in the Lamb's Book of Life and we're safe no matter what happens. We get the double benefit of experiencing the mind-blowing peace that God has for us now, and most importantly, the rock-solid assurance of a mind-blowing eternal experience.

God has proven his word to be accurate historically, scientifically, and prophetically; and will no doubt show itself to be accurate in the future. He wants us to experience the unshakeable rest for our souls from deep within until it's time to go home.

Jesus said:

> Come to me, all you who are weary and bur-
> dened, and I will give you rest. Take my yoke
> upon you and learn from me, for I am gentle and
> humble in heart, and you will find rest for your
> souls. (Matthew 11:28–29)

My hope for you and your family is that you'll come to Jesus with all your burdens, doubts, fears, and anxieties to experience the satisfying soulful rest that he has promised. We will not only have the assurance that our names are written in the Lambs Book of Life, but on the permanent guest list for the wedding party of a lifetime. If you are ready right now, pray this prayer after me and run to a life full of victory and purpose. Bet everything you have on red—for you will never lose.

> Dear Lord,
>
> Thank you for loving me and never giving up on me. Please forgive me of all my sins past, present and future. I've been living my own way and I want to change and give my life to you. I believe you died for me and rose from the dead to save me. Thank you in advance for hearing me, loving me and forgiving me. Lord, continue to bless me and help me live your way.
>
> In Jesus name, amen.

If you prayed that prayer, congratulations! You are now a child of God forever. Start by finding a Bible-believing church in your area and read his Word as much as you can, even if it's just for a few minutes at a time. Most importantly, talk to God as though he were your best friend—because he is. Share everything with him; he knows it all anyway. Be real with him and be yourself. He loves you just the way you are!

SPECIAL THANKS

I would like to thank those who have made a tremendous impact on my life.

My amazing wife and kids, Robynn, Emma, and Nate—the greatest blessings a husband and father could ever have.

My dad, Perry, who overcame substance abuse to be the best dad in the world.

My grandparents, Dinah and Bill, who rescued me from a troubled home.

My mom, Jamie, who is enjoying heaven as we speak.

My aunt Patty, who introduced me to God's love.

My mother-in-law, Jeri—Thank you for being an amazing grandmother and role model of selflessness.

My sisters, Nancy and Angel—I love you.

My brothers, Perry, Ronald, Ryan and Chris—I love you.

I would also like to thank Pastor John Van Schepen, who gave me the booklet that saved my life…my cousin Laura, who stuck with me during a crazy childhood…my bros, Rick and Rudy Torres, Richard Price, Lucas Davis, Mark Gould, Kevin Bass, Eddie Reay, and Keith Hall, who are always there to pray together and get through life's struggles together. I'd like to thank my second family, Bob Ross, Darlene, Michele, and Joey, who shared their home with me growing up and exemplified unconditional love. A huge thanks to our friends Wayne and Mary, Dan and Diana, Scott and Olivia and Ashley, Steve and Dana who shared the joys of parenthood and friendship together. Andre, Tami, and Cindy—thank you for your encouragement and friendship through the years.

Thanks to those who have taught me the Word of God for over twenty years and being an inspiration, as you shared God's love without fear from the public stage, Ravi Zacharias, Joey Buran, Jon Courson, Daniel and Autumn Katz, Greg Laurie, Erwin McManus, Brian Broderson and the late pastors Billy Graham and Chuck Smith.

Last, I would like to thank Andy Mineo, NF, Lecrae and the 116 crew, W.L.A.K, Sonny and the guys from P.O.D., Jeremy Camp, Thousand Foot Crutch, Rend Collective, Jesus Culture, Chris Tomlin, Mosaic MSC, and many more whose music has inspired me along life's journey. God bless you all!

ABOUT THE AUTHOR

Sunny southern California wasn't so sunny for Shawn in the early 1980s. He was born into a family riddled with alcohol, drug abuse, and frequent 9-1-1 calls to his early childhood home. Toward the end of Shawn's early childhood, his father broke the chains of addiction and became an amazing role model and hero, along with his grandparents, who took him in.

The reality of Shawn's broken childhood seemed to have a lasting effect. The unstable environment he called home for years, created a shadow of anxiety, fear of the unknown, and an emptiness that followed him. Through a series of amazing events explained in his book debut, *Betting on Red*, the veil of darkness that once hung over Shawn's life disappeared immediately, leaving behind an overwhelming peace and hope that flooded over his life. The rising tides of anxiety and negativity and eventual thoughts of suicide were washed away in an instant.

Shawn realized that the formula for his breakthrough was simple and easy to duplicate for anyone who was struggling as he was. He quickly developed a strong desire to begin writing and honing his ability to convey a simple yet powerful message for anyone looking to destroy the darkness in their lives.

Shawn currently lives in southern California with his beautiful bride of twenty years and two amazing children. Over the last several decades, he has been active serving his family, volunteering in church ministry, counseling with children that have cancer, helping the sick and injured as a firefighter/paramedic, serving as a volunteer for the developmentally challenged and as a coach for his son's elementary school sport teams. Walking with God and studying the Scriptures for almost two decades has led to Shawn's passion to spread peace, hope, and happiness in the lives of others around him.

CPSIA information can be obtained
at www.ICGtesting.com
Printed in the USA
LVHW041151171120
671900LV00005B/406

9 781098 031046